D0855569

My Dear Parents

My Dear Parents

THE CIVIL WAR SEEN BY
AN ENGLISH UNION SOLDIER

By James Horrocks

Edited by A.S. Lewis

HBJ

HARCOURT BRACE JOVANOVICH, PUBLISHERS

San Diego New York London

Library of Congress Cataloging in Publication Data

Horrocks, James, b. 1843.
 My dear parents.

 Includes index.
  1. Horrocks, James, b. 1843. 2. United States —
History — Civil War, 1861-1865 — Personal narratives.
3. United States. Army. New Jersey Artillery Batallion,
5th (1863-1865) — Biography. 4. United States — History —
Civil War, 1861-1865 — Participation, English. 5. Soldiers
— England — Biography. I. Lewis, A.S. II. Title.
E601.H79 1983   973.7'81   83-10717
ISBN 0-15-163674-5

Printed in the United States of America

First American edition

A B C D E

Editor's Note and Acknowledgements

As far as possible James Horrocks's letters have been transcribed as they have been written. Errors in dates have been retained, even where the rare wrong month or year has been used to date a letter. Any alterations have been limited to certain cases of spelling and punctuation to avoid confusion and to extend such abbreviations as Q.M. and Arty. Brid. to Quartermaster and Artillery Brigade in order to clarify meaning.

I would like to acknowledge the generous assistance I have been given by James Horrocks's niece, Mrs Dora Barrett, and his great-nieces, Mrs Brenda Ingham and Miss Joan Horrocks; also Mrs James Ratcliffe, Superintendent of Holland's Sunday School, Farnworth, for access to school records; Mr Howard Peters; Mrs Yvonne Ryden; the Archivists of Bolton and the Lancashire Record Office; the Libraries of Blackburn, Bolton, Farnworth, Guy's Hospital Medical School, St Louis, Trenton and the American Embassy in London; and especially the Borough of Blackburn and Lancashire County Council for their permission to reproduce the letters.

A. S. Lewis
June 1982

Contents

List of Illustrations

Introduction

WHEN JAMIE HORROCKS sailed for America in 1863 he was making an escape. Only a few months earlier a bright future for him in England had seemed assured. Now, at the age of nineteen, with barely the family to know his whereabouts, he was working his passage on a sailing ship from Liverpool bound for New York.

Back home in Farnworth a sixteen-year-old girl had become pregnant and, no matter how much James protested his innocence, a court of law, not to mention several neighbours, had declared that James Horrocks was the culprit.

It was a distressing time for the Horrockses at Farnworth where James's father, George, a local mill-owner, was a prominent member of the Wesleyan community.

Though well-established in Farnworth, George was not a native of the town. His roots lay a few miles further north, up in the hills between Bolton and Over Darwen. There his father had been a weaver in the deep, wooded valley of Bradshaw brook. George, with his wife Ann and baby Joseph, had moved higher up the valley from his father's home to Nicodean where he earned a living as a cotton-spinner. It was about 1843 when George with his wife and now three small sons, Joseph, William and Harry, moved the six miles downstream to Farnworth where he set up in partnership with the husband of one of his elder sisters, Bob Dearden, as a cotton-spinner and manufacturer. There in December 1843 the family's fourth child was born. This was James, the first of the sons to be born in their new home at Farnworth.

Farnworth, or Halshaw Moor as it was also known, was a small but fast growing community. A fair number of its new inhabitants were Irishmen. Its main industries, in addition to agriculture, were coal-mining and the manufacture of paper and cotton. Along the east side of the little town ran a newly opened railway line linking Bolton with Manchester. East of the railway flowed the winding

River Croal which was fed by the Bradshaw brook. Beyond the Croal stretched the canal to Bury and Manchester. In terms of communications Farnworth offered much greater opportunities than the banks of Bradshaw brook.

Horrocks and Dearden's new mill, Mount Pleasant, stood close to the northern end of Market Street, the high street through the town. A few hundred yards further north up that road lay Moses Gate railway station, on the main line to Manchester. The Horrockses made their home in Queen Street, close to the mill.

In the dozen years that followed the move to Farnworth, five more babies were born in the Horrocks home. There was George; next Annie, the only daughter in the house; then Walter, Peter and Benjamin. It was a tightly knit family and a happy one. George Horrocks was a father who liked to play and joke with his children and he took a lively interest in their education.

By 1851 the mill employed sixty-five hands and yet, within himself, George could feel a hankering for the open spaces. Unlike one of his sisters he could sympathise with his mother when, at the age of seventy and a widow, she pulled up her roots in about 1850 and emigrated with Henry, another of her sons, to Illinois.

Mrs Wright Greaves, George's sister, wrote her some unkind verses which began,

> Thou art growing old, mother,
> Thy locks are looking grey.
> Thy troubles hasten on, mother,
> Thy seventy years do say.

Another four verses go on to explain how her mother's eyes are growing dim and her teeth falling out before the poem closes with the lines,

> Then is it not in vain, mother,
> For thee to emigrate.
> Mere vanity of vanities,
> Ne'er think of Illinois State.

George, in contrast, wrote to his brother in America after a few years, "I have many a time had a good mind to come to you and Mother and Mary. If I had no family I should have come before now. I think I should like to have a nice farm upon a rich and fertile

12

piece of land but it appears my lot to be amongst machinery." As for the machinery, "I have many a time considerable pleasure after some extra exertion with some new machine or some newly repaired one to see it turn round and produce that which no mortal man can do by manual labour."

At the southern end of Farnworth's Market Street stood a Sunday school known as Holland's School. It had been founded in the early years of the century and was remarkable for being independent of any church denomination. The trustees, the daughters of its founder, Roger Holland, happened to be Anglican; the majority of the Sunday school's staff on the other hand were Wesleyan. George Horrocks served as a Visitor for the school. That is, he was responsible for checking up on pupils of the school when they were absent. It was a school that tried to offer more than religious teaching; although open only on Sundays, it attempted to give a general education.

Even so, the Wesleyans of Farnworth felt the need for a regular day school too. In 1853 a public subscription was opened for a school and in the following year a Mr Knox was appointed to be the schoolmaster. Both George Horrocks and Bob Dearden were to serve on its management committee.

In 1858 George, a big, strapping fellow, risked physical violence for the sake of his faith and its property. The Wesleyan chapel and the new school in Market Street stood alongside Jim Boardman's Horseshoe Inn. The building of a new wall on the chapel site upset the innkeeper's wife, Mary, who believed it was encroaching on her husband's land. She flew at George who happened to be standing on the chapel side of the wall but, losing her balance, fell backwards onto the rubble. She accused George of assaulting her. A court found there was no case for him to answer and George received the sympathy of the management committee at its following meeting.

Young James Horrocks attended both Holland's Sunday school and the new Wesleyan day school. Every New Year, Holland's School used to celebrate by holding a Tea-meeting. The children would be given a bite to eat and some tea to drink and selected scholars would give a recitation. Jamie's turn came in 1857 with a recitation entitled "A Mighty Cure All". Two of his companions giving recitations with him were John Nuttall with "A Happy New Year to You" and Richard Hamer with "No Pay No Work". The

13

same year at Holland's School saw James's elder brother, Harry, become a Sunday schoolteacher with Betsy Mort, a grocer's daughter from Dixon Green, a hamlet across the fields on the west side of town. Both James himself and John Nuttall became infant-teachers at the Sunday school a couple of years later in 1860, a crucial year. By this time George Horrocks had become one of the school's two superintendents. In the spring of 1860 the teachers threatened to withdraw en masse from the Sunday school on account of the continued refusal of the trustees to allow them to handle any funds to purchase new books. The problem was only solved by a founder's daughter providing money out of her own purse for the purchase of the books.

Like Holland's School, the Wesleyan day school relied upon senior pupils to assist with the teaching. Jamie Horrocks was almost made a pupil-teacher there as early as April 1857. His companion, George Thomas Duffy, was accepted but at sixteen he was three years older than James and it was felt that there were as yet insufficient children at the school for James's appointment to be justified. In the following year James was taken on as an honorary pupil-teacher and in 1859, with 200 children now attending the school, the indentures were signed for James to become a full pupil-teacher. He was paid for this work and, in addition, he used to earn a little extra in the evenings by calling from house to house to collect outstanding medical fees on behalf of the local doctor.

In those days both the Horrockses and Farnworth were in an expansive mood.

Joseph, Jamie's eldest brother, had left home to take up a post as clerk with the Lancashire & Yorkshire Railway Co. at their Over Darwen station. In September 1859 the second brother, William, set out for London with his father's blessing to study at Guy's Hospital Medical School to become a doctor. From his lodgings in Lambeth he conjured up, in a letter home, a nice description of the family, sitting by the fireside in Queen Street:

> Sometimes when I am thinking about home and its comforts I can picture you all round the fire talking things over, Father smoking, Mother looking a *black look* (beware Napoleon), Harry laughing as if half of his pate would come off, James looking rather sober but yet enquiring, George laughing, Annie pressing her lips

together and smiling, Walter just moving his head and looking consequential, Peter half asleep, Ben being rocked by Father, Tom cat sucking the old one on the dresser, all looking comfortable.

Henceforth William was to take a personal interest in the ailments of his family, including his father's leg which was beginning to give trouble.

The special event for Farnworth's Wesleyan community at Christmas 1859 was the opening of a public subscription to build a new chapel. George Horrocks of course was closely involved. The cornerstone was laid the following summer and George with Bob Dearden was among the thousand who turned up to take part.

James too was making strides. In February both he and George Duffy received promotion at the Wesleyan day school. George Duffy was someone he got on with. It was George who taught him to smoke. They used to go for walks and in June they took a long walk together to visit the new monument erected at Worsley to the memory of the Earl of Ellesmere. It was a tall tower with a winding stairway that led up to a rewarding view from the top.

That summer James took up the study of German, a language which his brother Joseph had already attempted to master. In the autumn he gave up his part-time job collecting fees for Dr Clarke, and began to attend a course of evening classes in Latin and Greek at Owen's College, Manchester. A friend of the family, Mr Gruber, was kind enough to help him with his Ovid. Mr Knox, the schoolmaster at Farnworth, was grooming James to make a career as a teacher.

The third brother was Harry. He took the whole of his family by surprise when he was spotted by Joseph, with his cousin James Dearden, on Bolton railway station wearing the slate-grey uniform of the 76th Lancashire Rifle Volunteers. Rifle Volunteer units were being raised throughout the country out of a recognition of the lack of any military reserve in Great Britain during the campaigns of the previous decade. There was some apprehension too over the current military ambitions of the French. In the event, the Volunteers' bands were to prove useful on major social occasions even if many of the recruits, like Harry, seemed to be only playing at soldiers and soon lost interest as the novelty wore off. His family agreed that Harry looked more handsome in his uniform than ever he had without it and seventeen-year-old Jamie upset his elder brother by secretly trying it on one Sunday while Harry was out.

At the beginning of 1860 the cotton trade was flourishing. George Horrocks was nominated to serve on a committee which would seek to improve the public amenities of Farnworth. There were plans afoot for new mills to be built. Prospects were good enough to persuade Harry to train at Mount Pleasant Mill for a career in mill-management. As William reminded his father, ". . . the trade of cotton spinning and manufacturing will never die out so long as children are born stark naked."

In Queen Street the Horrockses moved into Davenport House— Mr Knox the schoolmaster's old quarters. The summer was wet but Jamie did his bit by planting eighty celery plants in an attempt to improve the new garden.

By July trade was slackening but George, the greying head of the Horrocks household, had taken the bit between his teeth. For a long time his ambition had been to become the sole owner of Mount Pleasant Mill. In September two valuers visited the mill and, on the strength of their advice, Messrs Hinmer & Blacklock were persuaded to advance George a loan of £1,500 to purchase Bob Dearden's share of it. Negotiations dragged but at last, in November, George became the proprietor and all his family joined with him in his delight. In December when Thomas Barnes, M.P. for Bolton and owner of Dixon Green Mill, the biggest cotton factory in Farnworth, gave a party for one and a half thousand guests to celebrate his son's coming of age, George Horrocks was able to attend as the owner of Horrocks's Mill.

It was George's fate that events three thousand miles away were about to convert the greatest success of his working life into a personal tragedy. He had introduced new machinery into the mill for faster productivity, but the cotton mills of Lancashire were almost wholly dependent for their raw material upon the cotton growing southern states of the USA. By February 1861, the price of raw cotton had risen so high that it was devouring most of the profits and by March Bolton's mill-owners were having to consider imposing a five per cent reduction in their workers' wages. This was not going to be just a temporary recession caused by a downswing of the market. By the third week in March thousands of Bolton's mill-operatives were being put out of work.

16

In May George confided to his son William in London, "Our mind is a little troubled on account of the American war, getting cotton to such a high price, and what makes it worse we cannot see the end." In June he was barely able to make ends meet and in September told William, "I think I shall make all the cotton I have into money and stop entirely and wait as well as I am able for something better turning up." Bitter though this must have been, it was the best decision that George could have made. It saved him from slipping the whole way down the slope into bankruptcy.

Joseph fortunately gained promotion in October to become chief goods manager at Over Darwen railway station where he was put in charge of a workforce of nineteen, with nine horses and a dozen lurries. William was able to meet a large part of his expenses at Guy's by assisting a doctor in south London and Harry left Mount Pleasant Mill to work for a Mr Entwistle of Bolton, selling cigars. The three eldest sons were earning money. James, however, needed to train if he were ever to be made into a professional school-master.

His father was aware of the problem. If James were to be sent to the Wesleyan teachers' training college at Westminster, the Hor-rockses could look forward to two years in which they would have to continue to provide for his clothing and living expenses. At the end of three years James could expect to get a job as a schoolmaster earning a salary of about £80 a year. On the other hand, James's father could picture him now working at Manchester, making a living as a first-rate salesman.

It was Joseph who was convinced that Jamie should be encour-aged to go to training college. William, already in the metropolis, believed that being in London alone would do him good. Further-more Mr Knox, the schoolmaster, thought James was capable of winning a first-class scholarship. At the end of November James received a letter from Westminster College requesting him to be in London on the evening of 16th December in order that he might sit the entrance examination the following day.

In spite of the economic crisis there was something to celebrate in Farnworth that Christmas. On Christmas Eve the carol singers went round the town as usual and James went with them wheeling a harmonium. On Christmas Day, at the annual tea-party held in the Wesleyan day school, a presentation of two books was made to

James, and the chairman, Mr Brookes, gave a speech which lasted ten minutes, extolling James's virtues.

James won the first-class scholarship as Mr Knox had predicted and was invited to attend Westminster College when it re-opened after the Christmas break.

The Horrocks home was quieter when James had gone. It upset his mother. In the past she used to get annoyed at the noise James sometimes made playing the piano. Now she missed it and would mutter, "There is no Jimmy now and as for the piano it will never speak again i' th' world." In spite of the cotton slump, James was disappointed to find there had been more food on his plate at Davenport House than he was being served at Westminster College; this caused his mother to worry that he might not be getting enough to eat.

He was lucky in having a brother in London who was able to show him round town. He also quickly involved himself in the College's social activities. Scarcely a month there and he was singing a solo, "Kit the Cobbler", at a College concert. The regular amateur concerts were something he enjoyed. He learnt fencing. He took part in some fights. He also gained a reputation on the cricket pitch at Battersea Park where, in a game against the second years in May, he took seven wickets for nine runs. Afterwards he was chosen to play for the College team against St Mary's Roman Catholic College, Hammersmith. The marks for his studies were not bad but one of the most noticeable faults that the staff did find with him was his Lancashire pronunciation.

In August, when his revered brother Joseph came up to London, James took a delight in showing him the sights. In a single day, despite steady rainfall, the two attended a service in St Paul's Cathedral and visited Somerset House, Covent Garden, Drury Lane, Trafalgar Square, Horseguards and St James's Park. At Buckingham Palace they saw that all the blinds were drawn in mourning for the recent death of Prince Albert. After dinner they visited Westminster Abbey and the new Houses of Parliament, and they completed their tour with a trip to the Thames Tunnel.

In the summer, brother William passed his final examinations and, after three years of training, returned to Lancashire to set up a practice as a doctor in Edgworth. There he moved into Bank Cottage on the steep eastern slope of the Bradshaw brook valley, between his grandmother's old home at Vale House and his early childhood home of Nicodean. Harry now had a job working for the railway at Over Darwen station where his brother Joseph was anxious to get him an indoors promotion as a clerk. Even their younger brother George had found employment now as a merchant seaman.

It seems likely that, but for his family's financial difficulties at home, James would have gone on to become a teacher but, realising that his father could not afford to keep him a second year at Westminster College, Jamie began to look about for a permanent job. He would have liked to become a teacher but such posts were not easy to find even for students who had completed two years at the College. He wrote to the Admiralty, the Civil Service and even thought of going to Bengal, from where Indian cotton was being imported at a prodigious rate in an attempt to ease the shortage of American cotton for the mills. At the end of 1862 Jamie arrived home from Westminster College and he did not return there.

With Lancashire's economy dependent upon it, the course of the American civil war was being followed in the county with avid interest. The progress of the war received consistently more attention in the weekly *Bolton Chronicle* than any other news item.

Opinions in the district were distinctly divided. In January 1863, on one hand, the *Chronicle* roundly condemned the emancipation of the slaves as a clumsy ruse to encourage the southern slaves to rise up and assassinate their masters. In mid-February, on the other hand, an emancipation meeting was held at the Congregational Sunday school in Farnworth. Five hundred attended who, in addition to endorsing emancipation, expressed the need for the United States' continued unity in order to preserve the supply of cotton. The writer of a letter to the *Chronicle* claimed that never before had a public meeting in Farnworth excited so much interest.

The emancipationists were encouraged by the arrival in Lancashire in the same month of the United States vessel *George Griswold* bringing relief supplies to the distressed county, including seventy barrels of American flour for the Farnworth & Kersley Special Relief Committee. At the end of the month an anti-slavery meeting at the Temperance Hall in Little Bolton drew an attendance of two thousand and on 28th February the *Bolton Chronicle* printed a letter from a native of Eagley, a village north of Bolton, who was in America serving with the 7th Massachusetts Volunteers.

However the cotton needed for the mills was to be found not in the northern states but in the south. A small quantity was being brought out of southern ports aboard blockade-runners. News came at the end of March that six vessels had broken out through the blockade of Charleston to reach Nassau in the Bahamas. One of the ships bearing cotton was the *Hero* under Captain Peat. Several Farnworth businessmen had invested in her cargo. It was said that at Liverpool she was believed to be carrying eight hundred barrels of cotton; in Farnworth rumour exaggerated her load to twice the amount.

Both the factions in the American struggle could have discovered they had a number of supporters of Farnworth.

James was spending a great deal of time at Edgworth, at Bank Cottage, his brother William's new home. It was an attractive place to be. They had relations and friends close by. Downstream a few hundred yards, beyond the old Horrocks home, Vale House, lay the Jumbles, a wooded landscape bordering Bradshaw brook that was popular for picnics with visitors from Bolton. From the front door of the cottage, looking out across the valley, he could see the moors over Turton Heights rising high beyond the little Turton village. However, in making his way to Edgworth, James may well have been seeking a place to hide. The people at Farnworth he would have been trying to avoid bore the surname Hamer.

Richard Hamer, a railway clerk, had been at Sunday school with James. In 1857 they had both given a recitation at the New Year tea-party at Holland's School and both of them became teachers at that Sunday school. Richard's father had been manager of a print-works. He was long dead and Richard and Martha, his younger sister, lived with their mother in Barncroft Road, just around the corner from Queen Street.

Their elder sister, Selina, twenty-seven years old, had been the victim of a local scandal. She too was a teacher of long standing at Holland's Sunday school when she married James Leach, the school's assistant secretary and librarian. Soon after this, in January 1862, their peace and that of the Sunday school was rudely disturbed when a young lady named Alice Council announced that she was having an affair with Selina's husband. This affair had been going on before he was married but Alice claimed she was still involved with him. James Leach reluctantly had to resign from his position at the

Sunday school. Scandal had unfairly burst its way into the Hamer household and it was not going to go away.

Martha Jane was one of the youngest of the family. She was two years younger than her brother Richard and, like him, gave a New Year's recitation at the Sunday school. It was entitled "The Little Child on the New Year". She also attended the Wesleyan day school and there, like James Horrocks, she became a pupil-teacher. When she found herself pregnant in early 1863 the mill-owner's son, recently returned from Westminster College, was named as the father.

The folk James knew in Farnworth took sides for or against him. His brother Harry was a teacher at Holland's Sunday school and so was Harry's girlfriend, Betsy Mort. Betsy showed herself to be on Jamie's side. So did John G. Haas, with whom James had shared accommodation at Westminster College. Haas spoke up for his friend to the College Secretary, saying,

> James Horrocks has told me in deep sincerity he is as innocent of the alleged crime as either you or I are ourselves and until you can present me with stronger evidence than a mere girl's accusation I will and must consider him innocent.

In the early summer when Martha's case was taken to court to decide who should bear responsibility for the child's upkeep, judgement was found against James. Young George, his brother, on learning the result, wrote to his father from Cardiff where his ship was about to sail for the Bay of Biscay, "I have just received your letter and am very sorry about Bro. James and I think it is a shame for her that it is you and Mother must feel it I know but never mind. All I have to say is she is a B—ch."

Not everyone felt so sympathetic towards Master Horrocks. One who turned against him was his old companion from the day school, George T Duffy. In the winter of the previous year George Duffy's own younger brother, Robert, finding himself in a similar predicament, had had to marry his girlfriend, Emily, at a shot-gun wedding. The Duffys were fairly influential in the little town. The father, Henry, an Irish grocer from Sligo, was more an immigrant than the Horrockses but he had married the daughter of Robert Lawton, one of the respected elders of the community who, in the early days of

21

Farnworth's cotton industry, had worked with Thomas Barnes's father to get the Barnes factory into production.

Fortunately any ill will felt towards Jamie does not seem to have been extended much towards his family. In May George Horrocks was summonsed for failure to pay the lighting rates for his mill. He argued that his mill was no longer in operation and that legally it was in the ownership of the mortgage company. Although told to pay, he received a very sympathetic hearing.

William, a successful doctor in Edgworth, was, despite James's trouble, offered the assistant secretaryship and librarianship of Holland's School.

Meanwhile the campaign on behalf of the Yankee states was gaining momentum around Bolton. Andrew Jackson, an escaped slave who claimed to have been Jefferson Davis's coachman, toured the district in late June and early July attracting audiences in their thousands at Farnworth and Edgworth. By this time however James Horrocks was no longer in the neighbourhood to hear him. Not even a letter from John Haas inviting him to come away and stay with him in London arrived in time. Preferring exile to the responsibilities of a family or of paying for the upkeep of a child who he claimed was not his own, James had already embarked at Liverpool aboard a sailing ship bound for America.

Camp
Trenton
New Jersey
U.S.
Sept 5th 1863

My Dear Parents,

I was unsuccessful in obtaining a situation in New York and have enlisted in the 5th Battery New Jersey Volunteers (light artillery). This is about the best branch of the service as there will be no picket duty nor carrying knapsacks. I shall ride a horse and have very light work. The bounty is about the best that has been given yet. I shall get when muster'd in $200 from the state of New Jersey, 50 dollars from Hudson City (where I enlisted) and 25 dollars from the Government. This together with a month's pay in advance will make $288 cash down. In the paper I sent, you would see larger bounties advertised but I have enquired at nearly every place and find that the highest bounty paid down at once is $250 for a substitute. The Captain of our Company has made me Clerk to the Company. I shall get no extra pay for it but shall stand a good chance of promotion. I should have written before this but I thought I would defer it until I could send you the money—we have not yet been mustered in but expect to next week. I enlisted a fortnight ago and as I fully intend to desert if I don't get good treatment I enlisted under the name of Andrew Ross. I suppose if I remain the full three years here I shall have forgot who I am, and no one will be able to tell me. Very likely we shall proceed from Trenton, the capital of the state of New Jersey, to Washington and be drilled there about three months so that we shall not go into actual service before next spring, by which time everybody nearly says *the war will be over*. I doubt it. I shall be able to save more money as a soldier than as a clerk with 400 dollars a year (that is a pretty good salary in New York). I shall have 13 dollars a month besides the bounty, about 100 dollars of which I shall draw after I am discharged. I wish I could send you a photograph of myself in the uniform. I have a cap. . . . The trousers are light blue, double seated for riding. The jacket is dark blue trimmed with red. Besides these articles of dress I have two pairs of drawers, two woollen shirts, one pair of shoes, one

23

pair of Cavalry boots, a blanket and a loose coat with brass buttons like the jacket, a revolver and a sabre and a large overcoat complete my equipment. We have three meals a day—bread (no butter) and coffee in morning, soup, beef or pork, bread, potatoes or rice to dinner, and breakfast over again for supper.

I am in good health with the exception of a kind of rash that has broken out on my face, arms and legs. The doctor says it is caused by the heat of the weather and will go away of itself. I don't care how soon it does go away as it itches awfully sometimes.

I have left my trunk in the care of Mr Brady, 114 Cedar St., New York, where I lodged.

Sept 8th, Afternoon. The company has been mustered in today and I have received $250 in notes on the Trenton bank. The remaining 38 dollars will be paid in a few days. I intend by some means to send you £40 which will cost me at the present rate of exchange about 246 dollars. I shall have quite sufficient left for all my requirements and shall perhaps be able to send more by and by.

My skin has got nearly clear of the rash and I am very comfortable.

This is really a rich country even from the small knowledge I have of it. Besides the ordinary fruit you buy in England, here you can buy in abundance pineapples, watermelons, mush-melons, peaches, pumpkins and grapes quite cheap.

Yesterday I went down to the Delaware River about a mile from the Camp and had a nice bathe. Today I bought some fish tackle for 6 cents and went to fish. I caught 2 cat fish and an eel about 2½ feet long. The fellow who went with me used a different bait and caught quite a number of small fish something like English dace and perch.

*Aug 9th.** Last night I was ordered to go out with about a dozen men in order to catch deserters. The sergeant of the patrol put me and another trustworthy fellow to bring up the rear and we set out about 9 o'clock. Visited all the places in Trenton where it was likely we might be able to find them. We searched one or two houses of a certain character, greatly to the annoyance of certain happy couples who were unprepared to receive visits and then, after catching 12 of our men who were out on the spree (you must remember they had

*He means *Sept 9th.*

24

just received their bounty), we saw them safely ensconced in the guard house and went to have supper in one of the saloons. I had a jolly good blow out on the expense of the sergeant and another man, just as much as I could eat and drink for nothing. We remained there two hours and then strutted through the streets till three o'clock this morning. This morning I got a pass from the captain and went to the bank of Trenton to see if I could not get my paper exchanged into good looking English money. I found that in consequence of the high premium on gold and the rate of Exchange it would cost me about 7 dollars to the pound to get a draft on an English bank. (That is the way I intend to send you the money.) So I have made a deposit of 250 dollars in the Bank (The Mechanics and Manufacturers bank of Trenton, State of New Jersey) and intend to wait till the premium is lower before I get the exchange made.

I have sent one of the funny publications by post this morning, directed to Bro. Harry. By that and the paper I sent to Bro. Joseph you will perceive the state of feeling indulged towards the English in America.

Write as soon as you can and address to:

Andrew Ross
Care of Captn Z. C. Warren
5th Battery of New Jersey
Camp Perrine
Trenton
New Jersey, U.S.
or Washington, or elsewhere.

It is pretty certain that our Battery will not see active service before next spring and even then I expect to keep myself pretty secure and safe. The Company I am in is a motley assembly—Irish, Germans, French, English, Yankees—Tall and Slim, Short and Stout. Some are decently behaved and others uncouth as the very d—. I won't try to spin this out any longer but with best love to you and every member of the family, to Miss Mort, Coz Rachel and Old Haas. Believe me to be your sober minded, careful, steady and affectionate son,

James Horrocks

5th New Jersey Battery
Camp Perrine
Trenton, N. Jersey, U.S.
Sept 16th 1863
My Dear Parents,

Having nothing else to do I take up my pen again, to let you know how I get along. My convenience for writing is not very good so that I cannot write very long with comfort. You may be surprised at this after telling you that I had been made "Company clerk" but the fact is that office is almost a nonentity now that the company is mustered in and the muster rolls made out etc. I have nothing to do in the way of keeping accounts or at least very little and therefore take drill with the other men. I like it well enough. The only thing I find unpleasant is having too much time on my hands. It makes me dull occasionally. I have today got a book on Artillery Tactics which will help the time to glide along rather more pleasantly and profitably. I have no wish to desert yet. One of our deserters (we have a considerable number already) was caught a few days since. He lost his bounty or rather what he had left of it, about $200 by Confiscation, his head was shaved and he is placed upon a gun carriage every day with the word *deserter* on his back in Capitals. One of our men was killed by the railway cars the day before yesterday. He had got enough liquor to make himself dull and stupid (not sharp fresh) and sat down on the railway which runs alongside the camp. There was nothing uncommon in that, but when the train came rushing along, screaming and whistling to warn him, the man seemed asleep and although the engine driver did his best to stop the train and some of our men ran to save him, it was too late; in a few moments his head lay by the side of the rails and his body entangled in the wheels was carried about 30 yards further and there left the most shockingly mangled body one can imagine. His friends were telegraphed for to Nova Scotia. Yesterday we buried him in the cemetery with military Honors. Two companies followed his body to the cemetery marching in time to the brass band playing a dead march. Three volleys were fired over his grave and such was the end of one soldier.

Sept 19. I have just received your long delayed but most welcome letter. I can tell you I devoured the contents most eagerly. I am very glad Bros. Walter and Peter wrote and if I don't answer their letters personally I hope they won't fail to write again. Whenever I receive a letter from one of the family I feel as if it came from *the family* collectively and I answer with the feeling that I am writing at once to every individual member of the happy circle, united in love, to which I belong. It is my fervent hope and belief that the bonds of love and concord which has always been a distinguishing feature of our family may never be broken. When I enlisted I did not tell any of the gentlemen who had read my letters of introduction so in order to make sure of the letter which I had told you to direct to Messrs Arkell Tufts & Co. I wrote to Mr Arkell requesting him to forward your letter, of course I enclosed the price of postage and a directed envelope to myself. This he has very kindly done and I have received it safely. You need to be under no apprehensions as to the safety of any letters addressed to me. Soldiers' letters are taken as much care of in the States as in England and if our company has removed from here to any other place your letter will be sent after me.

I am very glad Bro. Joseph enjoyed himself so much. He just went about his pleasure seeking like an enlightened son of Freedom. One with a narrow contracted mind could not possibly have made as much of such a short holiday as he did. I was much amused by reading the account of "Poor Uncle Bob" as well as with Walter's and Peter's account of the bathe they had at Southport. A stranger reading Peter's letter would understand that Henry swam ½ mile and Peter ¼ of a mile. If such is really the case I must feel particularly astonished. It seems to me there has been a great deal going on since I left. Of course you will congratulate Coz. Rachel and her happy husband in my name. I wish them well and shall be extremely proud to hear that their union has been blessed by the birth of a smiling cherub. (*Strictly private*!!! If dear Robert Wood is *uncapeless* of the said manufacture of a little cupid, Andrew Ross is the chap that ain't—of course such an expression is inexcusable only in the way of consolation to Dear Rachel.)

It was impossible to send you word when I left Liverpool as the sea was so rough when the steam tug left us no letters could be sent on shore. I am sorry that mother was so anxious about me, as father would tell her that the ship might be 6 weeks on the voyage. She was exactly 40 days as *Harry* said she would be. As to the cooking for the 600 passengers, that is one reason why I so much preferred my own position. There was a galley on purpose for the cooking of their own provisions. Every one or every set as the case might be had pots and pans of their own for cooking purposes and they had to cook for themselves under the supervision of two men who only paid half fare, and made up their passage by looking after the passengers. In the galley was a large kind of oven with a fire in it, and holes on the top with lids. One part was a real oven for baking purposes but the principal part of their food was cooked over these holes in pans. Once a week provisions were served out to them—some rotten potatoes, salt meat, sugar, rice, flour and meal, enough to last 3 days with careful management. Most of them brought provisions from Ireland to make up the balance but many were half-starved before they got to New York. I always—or rather *we the boys*—had always a good deal of food left at every meal provided for us by the ship's cook and we regularly gave such over-plus to the half-starved, half-naked wretches whom we knew to be in necessity. A young woman came to me one day and asked me for the love of heaven to give her a potatoe or a biscuit to keep her from starving. I gave her what I could spare and so won her heart that at night when the passengers were sent below she absolutely invited me to go below and sleep—I need scarcely tell you that I did not accept her invitation. I would not own a fellow who would take such shameful advantage of a girl. I know I was a general favorite on board ship, but one morning when we had been washing the decks, the Captain and all the sailors laughed at my torture when the first mate sent me up to loose the mizen royal. I was in a pickle I can tell you. I suppose he sent me up for the fun of the thing. My feet were bare and tender with being in the water and it made me grin to walk up the ratlines, but I did it and then instead of coming down the same way I swarmed or slurred down a rope connecting the top of the mizen royal with the deck, 200 feet I should guess. One great privation the passengers used to suffer was want of water. Every morning they came and each received in turn 3 quarts of water from the carpenter. One would think 3 quarts enough on board ship but I assure you I have been offered sixpence for a drink of it. I was restricted nominally to 3 quarts a day but could always get as much as I wanted from the carpenter. It seems surprising to me that these poor Hibernians should think they are saving something by coming over in a packet ship for £3.10s. and then having to bring with them provisions and cook it themselves, and be 40 days on the passage—when they might come from Liverpool or Cork for 5 or 6 guineas, have 3 meals a day ready cooked for them and get to New York in much less than half the time, and they can get a drink of water any time. If a man has plenty of time and money I should advise him to sail as a 1st Class Cabin passenger on board a sailing vessel. There is nothing pleasanter when the wind blows fair than being on deck. No smoke or noise of engines, no evidence of the movement of the vessel, only the sails swollen out and the foam of the sea in the wake of the vessel.

I think I now ought to answer some of the enquiries of Peter and Walter as to what sort of houses and people and weather there is here. Well in New York the houses are very much like those of Liverpool. But here and out in the country generally all the houses are built of wood. They are very pretty and as far as I can see very comfortable to live in. As to the people a long letter might be filled up describing them. They are of so many different kinds. Irish seem to be as numerous as any other kind. A great many of them sell whiskey of their own make which has got the name of "Jersey Lightning". In Hudson City, where we were encamped first, nearly all the people are Germans. In fact there are a very large number of Germans everywhere I have been yet. They are awfully fond of a drink called "Lager bier". There is not much difference between that and ale.

In Greenwich St., N.Y., you may walk 200 yards down one side and every other shop is a Lager bier saloon. The Americans are a very sociable people, very good natured and hospitable, such has been my short experience of them. As I have mentioned the drinks of two classes of people I may as well tell you something of American drinks. Yankees are ingenious and in the mixture of spices and Liquor they have exercised their ingenuity to some purpose. These are a few names of said mixtures: Gin Sling, Milk Punch, Brandy Smash, Egg Nogg, Mint Julip, Gin Cocktails etc, etc. I have tasted a few of these but the best of all is the Sherry Cobbler. Sherry wine, some plantation bitters and spices are mixed together and put in a tumbler with ice, lemon and a few strawberries floating on the top. A straw is then given to you and you suck up the delicious fluid at leisure. As nearly all the gentlemen wear moustaches, this straw sucking is very convenient. I have a very decent black moustache myself. Don't be afraid of me becoming addicted to drink amidst such temptations. I have seen too much of its evils, I think, ever to forget myself. There is very little coal used for fuel here. Even the railway engines use logs of wood.

Our food is cooked over log fires . . . my dinner is being cooked now while I am writing. We are living in wooden cabins fitted up with sleeping bunks in the same way as on board ship. We sleep two in a bunk. An Irishman named O'Brien is my mate. He spreads his blanket in the bunk and we have mine over us at night. We don't have any straw under us, nothing but the bare boards. This is called a *barracks*. A human stable is a more proper name to give it. it. Another class of people are the niggers, who are undoubtedly considered by many if not most of the Yankees as an inferior species of animals to themselves. There was a case in the paper a few days since of an Irishman charged with having assaulted a Yankee. He admitted the charge, but justified himself on the ground that the Yankee had said, "A Nigger was as good as an Irishman." I don't know what the decision of the Court was. From what I have come to know of the Irish in this country it is a settled thing in their minds that before long they will go over to Ireland and liberate the country from the English yoke. One of them showed me a book of poetry entitled *The Spirit of the Nation* containing songs, some of them well written, and all expressing treason to the English government— such songs as The Green Above the Red, Down With the English Tyrant, etc. As I told you before the weather here has been extremely hot but about a week since a change took place for the better and we are now enjoying the most delightful weather. Neither too hot or cold but that kind of delicious atmosphere which gives new vigour to a man, and invites him to walk out and enjoy Nature.

*Aug 21.** I have been out myself today. I went as far as the Delaware which runs near Trenton. This is the River on which Philadelphia is built. Here it is broader than the Thames at Putney and moderately sized vessels sail up and down. I walked along the bank a while and then turned to the left, through a corn field. The stalks of corn were about 7 feet high and thicker than my thumb. Don't be astonished. It was Indian corn. I next went through a field of water melons, which grow and look like cucumbers, only they are about as large as
*He means *Sept 21*.

30

Jim Boardman's head. I next came to an uncultivated swampy place thick with vegetation of great variety. Amongst other things which attracted my attention was a plant bearing a kind of pod which, on cutting up with my knife, I found to contain a silky substance which struck me at once as being fit for making into cloth. I met a Yankee looking fellow with a broad straw hat and asked him what sort of a plant he called it and he coolly told me it was cotton and so spoiled the visionary dreams I had of introducing a new thing into the world to take the place of cotton. Of course this was wild but it seems to me to be of a very superior kind. I enclose you half the contents of one of these pods. One thing that I noticed both here and in Hudson County (where we were encamped last) was the immense number of butterflies, grasshoppers and locusts. I am not sufficiently acquainted with botany to tell you about the trees here but it is easy to see they are many of them different to anything we have in England.

Sept 22nd. It is rather cold today. I think we shall have rain. It never rains here I think like it does in England, drizzling on for days together, but goes ahead with a right good will coming down in torrents for about 24 hours or less, and then stopping altogether for a fortnight perhaps. I will send you a draft for £20 when I send this off as I think father can make use of it and although by waiting a month or two I might save something if the premium on gold came down still I am not certain of this and in the meantime it might form an increasing nucleus in father's pocket. I would send it all as I mentioned in my last but there is a possibility of me getting a lieutenant's commission and if so I shall want some money at once for an outfit. I say there is a possibility of it as every man has an equal chance of promotion and the Captain seems to like me very well. He is only about 24 years of age and if he makes me a sergeant I won't be long before I get a commission. There is no telling—I may be able to send you a ship load of Cotton yet: Depend on it I will look after it Damned sharp.

Sept 23rd. I have just been to the bank at Trenton and got a draft on London for 20£ which you will be able to get cashed in Manchester. It cost me 140 dollars. I have still 130 dollars in my pocket besides having bought a nice pair of boots for 6½ dollars and a few other articles of comfort. I have it in Greenbacks which is about the best and safest money in currency here. There are hundreds, nay thousands of different kinds of bills in currency and Greenbacks are the most difficult to forge. There are small bills in circulation for 5 cents, 10c, 25c, and 50c. 25 cents is called 2 shillings, thus making an American shilling equal to 12½c or 6¼d. Greenbacks are one dollar or 2 or 3 or 5 or 10, 20, 50 or 100. I will post you the *N.Y. Herald* for today at the same time as this letter. This paper is the great leader of the Democratic Party. The *Tribune* is the leader of the Republican. Uncle Henry's definition of the two is the right one.

I sincerely hope father is now quite well. I am thankful to say I am in good health and hope you are the same. I was much pleased to hear of sister Annie going to Southport as well as the rest of the youngsters. Brother Joseph's good luck at the Bazaar beats Creation. I hope Brother William is beating everybody else in the way of getting cash and fame and that Bro. Henry will not be long before he is getting money. And last I sincerely hope my dear Mother is quite well and contented in her mind about me. I assure you I am as right as a clock.

This is a decent length for one letter so I will now conclude as before with best love to all the family including Miss Mort and kind remembrances to W. Sutcliffe and my old friend Haas if you hear from either. I remain

Your very affectionate son,
James Horrocks

P.S. Please answer this at once and then I shall be set at rest with regard to the £20.

Washington
Oct 20th 1863

My Dear Parents,
I received Bro. Joseph's letter dated Septr. 27th yesterday but before I proceed to answer it I must first tell you how I have been going on since I left Trenton. We left that place on the very day you wrote the letter. We had knapsacks strapp'd on our backs containing all the property we had in the world or supposed to have. Most of the men were half tight or more properly were very loose in consequence of the whiskey they had swallowed, and as they

marched along the dusty road to the depot or Railway station enlivened the natives by singing various hymns such as Lanningan's Ball, and another called Glory Hallelujah!!!

> John Brown's Bollucks lies a dangling in the air
> *Ditto*
> *Ditto*
>> As we go marching along.
>> Glory, Glory, Hallelujah etc.

> Old Abe Lincoln stands shaking in his boots
> *Ditto*, *Ditto* and *Ditto*, Chorus.

We got on the cars about ½ past 6 in the evening. They are much wider and longer than those in England as you may imagine when they run on 12 wheels each. The platform is at the ends of the cars in the Omnibus style instead of along the sides and you can walk the whole length of the train if you think proper. The seats are movable and hold two persons but are arranged so as to leave a passage along the centre of the car.

The first thing that drew my attention on the journey was the river Delaware which flows near the railway the greater part of the way from Trenton to Philadelphia. It is a really beautiful river and as the moon shone brightly about ½ past 7, the scene was very pleasant. On the opposite bank the ground is undulating and decorated with numerous pretty wooden farms and copses of various kinds of trees. The vessels and rafts sailing alongside us all helped to make up the picturesque, but by and by we lost sight of the river and next found ourselves passing through the main street of a small town with shops on each side and people passing along.

We arrived at Camden Town at ½ past 9 and got off the cars and crossed over the Delaware to Philadelphia, a town very much like Liverpool in appearance, with its large warehouses facing the river. Here we were led to a fine saloon provided by the ladies of the city and set out with all the necessaries of a good supper, coffee, bread and butter, cheese, beef, ham and fruit etc. (The last means salt, pepper, mustard, vinegar and catshup.) We left Philadelphia at 11 o'clock and I had got comfortably seated in a corner of the car with a comrade, whose name is George Gordon de Lima Byron, who holds the rank of Corporal but notwithstanding that I fully believe that he is the only son of "Lord Byron". Don't laugh. I will tell you more of him by and by. Well as I was about to say I felt a kind of pleasant drowsy feeling come over me and I fell asleep, but at one o'clock Byron (*Lord*) wakened me up to see a little of Yankee Go-a-headism. We had arrived at Havre-de-Grace on the banks of the Susquehana and were about to cross it. I said the Delaware was a beautiful river but this looked magnificent. The water was perfectly smooth and seemed quite as broad as the Mersey at Liverpool but what surprised me was the way we went over. The *whole train* ran on the steamer in two parts and was *carried across*, and then went on its way screaming and rejoicing and well it might.

We arrived at Baltimore about 3 o'clock on Sunday morning and slept on the floor of a room belonging to the soldiers' relief association. We had a good breakfast there and set out for Washington at 8 o'clock. I think it was about 10 or half past when we came in sight of the city. The object that first struck my attention was a building very much resembling St Paul's Cathedral which Byron told me was the Capitol, or the House of the American Parliament. We marched from the station to this camp where I am now writing about 2 miles and found that no tents could be got for us that day, so we were compelled to sleep on the ground that night with the blue canopy of heaven stretched over us. On the next day we got our tents and pitched them, and the day after commenced a regular course of Drill, for this is a Camp of instruction for Artillery and there are here at present about 12 full batteries besides ours.

Our Battery is not a full one, only about 100 men instead of 150 and 4 guns instead of 6. They are brass 12 pounders and are available at 1,500 yards distance with shot and shell and 600 yards with canister. We have got our guns since we came here. Each gun or piece consists of two parts—the "limber" running on the first two wheels, and the cannon on the last two. For travelling these are coupled together, but are separated in action. The limber is merely an ammunition chest. Six horses draw the cannon and six the caison or ammunition carriage, of which there are four. Besides these every sergeant has a horse to himself and there are four horses to each battery wagon. Altogether there are about 80 horses for us to take care of. I am a driver now and have charge of two spirited horses. I guess I shall be a good horseman before long. I have only had charge of the horses a few days and cannot give you much account of my equestrian performances yet. The most important point I notice is the soreness of a soft part of my body with riding the brutes down to water.

I was very impatient last week about receiving a letter from home till on Sunday I was pacified by receiving a note from the P.O. Washington saying that a foreign letter was waiting there for me, to come with 36 cents for postage. I need scarcely say I should be willing to pay twice the sum for a letter from home. Well very fortunately I had got a pass for Monday to go into the city, so I went and first made my way to the P. Office (which is as fine a building almost as the London Post Office) and got my letter which half a glance at Bro. Joseph's well known writing told me was from HOME. I went right across the road to the Patent office which is an exhibition of all the Patents taken out by Yankees. I sat down in a nice place and read my letter, and now before I go any further let me say it will be better for you to pay the postage next time and then it will come straight on to me without me having to fetch it.

You seem to think your first letter never got to me but I expect by this time you have received my last letter, which was in answer to the one copied by father from the letter written by Bro. Joseph about his Isle of Man visit etc and in which I enclosed a draft on Geo. Peabody & Co., London, by Alex. Drexel & Co., Philadelphia, for 20£. If you have not received it write at once and let me know and will send you a duplicate of the draft with which you can draw the money.

I have not written to anyone in England, only you, since I left and if you wish to represent me as clerk for a travelling gentleman you can do so. It will be best. But with regard to that I must say that the Captain has played me false in that respect and has gradually made me into an ordinary member of his Company.

Byron tells me that there is no such position as Company clerk to a Battery. If this is so I think I ought to have my discharge, for the Captain has induced me to enlist under false pretences. I will look after myself in first rate style as Cap. Z. C. Warren will find. The reason I defer writing to the Colonel to represent my case is that I am learning horsemanship, and am not very badly off, and for another reason which you may think me simple to put any faith in. Byron who is a man of 54 years of age has been both a Major and Colonel in the American army on General Fremont's staff. But when Fremont was discharged, he too with all the staff was discharged. Since then he has been going down the hill very fast, having two or three children with his wife to take care of and keep. In fact his necessities were so pressing he enlisted and took the bounty in Jersey City, explaining his position to the Captain and intending to see Secretary Seward or Stanton and recover his rank or at least another commission. This he intends to do in a few days when he has recovered from an attack of the lumbago and when he has got it he promises to get me *out of this altogether*.

As near as I can recollect from his story, Byron was born in Cadiz in Spain, his mother, the Marchioness de Lima, having been privately married to Lord Byron when he was quite a young fellow. Lord Byron left her and in England married again to Miss Sinclair (?). He did this with impunity as a marriage with a Roman Catholic by an English peer in a foreign country is invalid, but some time after this marriage, the marriage with the Marchioness became known to her (his English wife) and she separated from Lord Byron and never lived with him again. You may remember that the reason of the separation of Byron and his wife is generally only guessed at by his biographers. Byron wrote a poem about this time dedicated "To My Son". This Byron my friend affirms to be to himself. I cannot tell you the whole story of Byron as he told it to me but he has been in Every part of the World and almost speaks English, French, Spanish, Italian and Persian. He has been Major in the East India Co.'s service. He has shown me his documents which prove him to have been in their Service about 20 years, as well as his American commissions. He is no imposter, as the Captain of our Company and several of the men knew him when he was Major Byron. But you will naturally ask how is it that he does not step forward and claim the title and property of Lord Byron. The reason is that the entail has been cut off and if he succeeded in raising £5,000 or £6,000 to put forth his claim, he might fail to get what he wants and if not there would be very little real benefit to him by it. Some years ago he contemplated the publication of a work to be entitled *The Inedited Works of Lord Byron*, Now First Published from his Letters, Journals, and other Manuscripts in the Possession of his Son, Major George Gordon Byron. But the Lord Chancellor granted to the Executors of Lord Byron an injunction to forbid its publication as they claimed the copyright of most of the letters. But as the Major had spent a great deal of money and many years of his life exclusively to the collection of these manuscripts and copies of manuscripts, he was determined not to be done and he published the work in America, intending to issue it in monthly parts to be completed in four volumes. Such a work with such a title could not fail to make a great sensation. It was such a surprise that the papers took it up and in most cases hinted that the letters etc were spurious and only got up by the bastard son of Lord Byron to make a sensation.

Major Byron made a very able defence, which I have been just reading, as well as the first part of the Publication. But the public had become doubtful and the result was that the number of copies sold was found to be not enough to make it pay. I should very much like to have Bro. Joseph see the work, or at least the portion of it that was published by Martins, New York, and which I have read.

Well now I cannot go on any further about him here but will tell you why I chose such a Scotch name as Andrew Ross. In the first place I did not wish it to be known in Yankee doodland that a real live Horrocks had condescended to enlist as a private in their confounded Gall Darned army and secondly if ever I desert and it was suspected by anyone who came to know me, I could prove that my name was James Horrocks and never had been Andrew Ross and that no such person had ever honoured them by going to be shot at for their sake. The English are very unpopular here and so are the Irish even more so (this is my impression) but the Scotch are a sort of go-between that the Yankees have no particular spite against, ergo—I become—Andrew Ross.

Quod erat Demonstrandum. Excuse the Latin. It's your own fault I am such a scholar.

Set your mind at rest with regard to my box. I left nothing in it that could tempt Mr Brady to sell it and I am sure I can get it if I like at any moment.

I guess Our noble English Rifle Volunteer, Harry "Ox", would be well able to obey those graphic and elegant commands: Eyes Backurts, Ass Upparts, Neaw Ross on that Cart Hass *Tention*, *Grab Tails*. But if he heard the commands in this service he might be a little puzzled to do it all in Double quick time, as it has to be done. We have no such thing as Common time in the *Mounted* or flying artillery. When the men and horses are all ready for action you hear such commands as these: Cannoneers prepare to Mount! Mount!!! Drive on!! Halt. Cannoneers prepare to Dismount. In Battery!! Limber up, Action to the rear. Load by Detail. Load two, three, four. Sponge two, three, four. Ram two, three. Ready! Fire!!! Fire to the right etc, etc. All the time every man is going through a different kind of work. Horses gallop round with the limber at the commands, In Battery, Action Rear or Front or Right as *the case may be.*

While in Washington on Monday I went into the Capitol both in the House of Senate and House of Representatives. They are very fine but not quite as splendid as our Houses of Parliament, although they are built of a more durable material, namely of marble all complete. I also went into the White House or Residence of the President.

I went into a Photographers and got my likeness taken for Cartes de Visite. I paid $1.50 for 6. I enclose you one (I received them by post today, 22nd.) If you want another I will send it to you.

You say my life appears to be full of adventure and romance. I think so myself, when I begin to think about it. If anyone could have the famous glass of the Necromancer and see me in the various positions I have been in it would seem rather romantic. Two years ago I should appear in the capacity of Pedagogue teaching the young idea in the farmers' village of Halshaw Moor. In the month of December that year I appear as a candidate for Queen's Scholarship being examined in London. Next as a successful competitor I am an inmate of the Wesleyan Training College. In the course of 12 months I am at home for the holidays and am no longer a fellow that no one need be ashamed of but become avoided by former friends, with a few exceptions. Next I appear in the Court of Justice or Injustice as the case may be, the observed of all observers and the talk of a whole neighbourhood. (But I forget a certain point and that is I become a clerk in a Cotton Mill.) Next I am a sailor standing on the yard of the Main Royal, out of sight of Land. Next I appear as a gentleman at Large in the city of New York, and to crown all I am now a soldier in the American army driving two horses etc, but in good health and spirits.

Well I must now try and wind up this letter or I shall never be able to get it posted. I send you *Frank Leslie's Budget of Fun.* As you anticipated I have never received a newspaper yet but have sent you several. Very likely I should get it if you sent me one now to my present address:

Andrew Ross
Care of Captn. Z C Warren
5th Battery, New Jersey
Camp Barry
Washington D.C.
U. States of America

I should like *Punch* and the *Bolton Chronicle*. I am glad Bro. William is doing well and hope he will find time to write me a letter. Bro. George will see a great deal of the world I dare say before he is 21. I have no doubt he will be a rich man sometime.

But of all countries in the world I think America is the easiest for a man to get a living in. It is not the difficulty of earning my bread that made me enlist but the desire to get money quick. A common labourer out West can get 2 dollars a day.

How would it be do you think for me to go to Illinois and see how the folks there are going on? I can get a pass at Christmas to go to N. York and could go from there to Cincinnati and from there to Illinois and once there I defy the whole government of the States for finding me out, and if the worst came to pass and I was caught, they would not shoot me because although I am a soldier I am not a conscript nor a substitute but a *volunteer*, and I should not be considered a deserter of the worst kind because we are not yet got into service. There have not been any shot except those who have deserted from the front of the enemy. There's another thing about it. I don't think the Yankees had any right to enlist me, an alien under age, without consent of my parents. But leaving all these considerations out of the question, I feel very determined not to risk getting even a scratch in this war. Of course as you say it would be different if I was fighting for my own country.

We have had fifty deserted out of this Company and only three of the number have been caught. Two of these have escaped again and the other one has only got his head shaved and put to hard labour for a few months. Just consider this a good sample of the Federal army, 50 deserters out of 150 men.

I should like very much to have the Carte de Visite of all the family or at least of Father, Mother and Bros. Joseph, William and Henry and sister Annie. I suppose Bro. George could not get his taken very conveniently. I have got the likeness of the younger part of the family.

I find it takes longer for a letter to come from England to America than from America to England. I think it is almost time I should receive an answer to my last letter.

Today is Saturday, Oct 24th. We have had no rain for a fortnight although in the month of October but today it rains very fast in consequence of which we stay in the tents and do very much as we please instead of going out to drill.

When I was in Washington on Monday I saw a placard in a Confectioner's shop window which almost threw me into a perspiration with astonishment. It was this: EVERTON TAFFY. I rushed in and asked the terrified shopman how he sold it. He tremblingly answered 30 cents a pound. Give me half a pound said I. He did so and I asked him if he made it himself. He said Yes. Then said I, you are selling a spurious article. He seemed to be groping in the dark till I explained to him that real Everton Toffy, not Taffy, must necessarily be made in Everton. I found the toffy very good.

I think I have made up a very long letter and hope you will try to do the same. I dare say I have not been very complete in certain parts but any questions that you may naturally ask about Byron, or anything else I have told you, I will try and answer in my next letter.

And now with kind remembrances to the very few I care about out of our own family, Miss Mort, Haas and William Sutcliffe and family, but not a word to the delectable families of Duffy and Hamer save this. They may go—oh. They may go—oh. They may go to the—for me, and with best love to all our family, believe me as ever

Your most Affectionate son,
James Horrocks

Monday, Oct 26th. I will post this letter this afternoon and then it will leave New York for England on Wednesday. I enclose the photographs of two of our Company.

I think I will take Bro. Joseph's advice and keep an occasional diary if not a regular one.

Try to send a very long letter in answer to this, and send it soon. It is one of the greatest pleasures I have or can have to receive a letter from home. I hope while this is on the way to you there is one from you on the way to me. We can always have it so, if you answer every letter of mine. That is if they don't miscarry.

Today there will be a grand review of the whole artillery here by General Barry. Every company will be in heavy marching order, just as we should be if we were marching to the enemy. As I told you before, it will be spring before our battery can possibly be ready for service.

There is more practice and science required in the Artillery Service than in any other.

Andrew Ross

                                        Camp Barry
                                        Washington D.C.

My Dear Parents and My Dear Bro. Joseph,

Today the 28th of Oct. I have received your letter dated Oct 11th.

There was no stamp on the letter but I received it without having to pay anything. How that is I do not know. But I suppose the Post Office Authorities in Washington let it slip instead of detaining it for the postage dues. I am very glad that you have received the letter containing the £20, and still more so that the money came so opportunely for father.

It was only yesterday I sent off a letter to you. It is quite unlucky that I did not defer it another day and then I could have acknowledged the receipt of this letter of yours.

Your advice with regard to desertion is good and sensible. One country is already too hot for me and I have left it. It is scarcely advisable to risk my liberty in this country and I shall therefore play my cards in such a style that I may get my discharge or a promotion as soon as possible. Perhaps I may fail in both. Well! Never mind, it won't break my heart. *No fear.* I can stand hardship as well as anyone I am acquainted with. What little I have had has only served to make me stronger and more hardy. Thank God and my parents for a good constitution.

If those strong gigantic fellows, G. T. Duffy and Johnny Nutto, were here I bet my month's pay they would be down ill with the Fever and ague or Dysentery like many others of such a breed.

Poor Old Byron is laid up from the effects of sleeping in a wet blanket but I hope he will soon recover and get his commission. He told me yesterday that if his health permitted he would have me *out of this* in four weeks. But he will have to get himself out of it first and get well. Let us hope he will succeed in both.

Such accidents as the one you mention in the Crowbank are very shocking. My mother's action in that matter only shows the genuine kindness of her disposition. I can remember when scores came begging to our door she would always hear their tale of woe and give them at least kind words and nearly always something to relieve them. She certainly has been as good as a mother to me and I will if possible take her advice for my own sake as well as hers and return to her safe and sound sometime.

Bro. Ben's note was very good. Tell him I should dearly like to see mother's new bonnet and that silk dress of Sister Annie's. But I hardly know what to say with regard to the execution of those innocent kittens. I really cannot believe he would be cruel to dumb animals but a thought strikes me that their death warrant was issued when he was standing on his head.

Bro. Peter's letter was very interesting. His regular attendance at the sunday school is very pleasing. I hope he will earn the 10/-.

Bro. Walter's letter was just as pleasant to read as the rest. I hope if Mr Knox does put him to any examination in Edinburgh or elsewhere, he will show himself to be superior to any other boy in the school. Read plenty of books and do as you are told, Walter. My father's and Bro. William's success gives me unbounded satisfaction. I think if we all pull one way we shall be rich sometime.

Nov 5th, 1863. Today is the time I suppose the youngsters will be bothering for "thrakle cake un towfy", the most approved method of celebrating the brunfire plot.

The Corporal of our detachment is an Englishman and celebrates the day as being the anniversary of "Inkerman" by wearing on his jacket French and English medals of the Russian Campaign and the Victoria Cross with Silver bars (almost if not quite the greatest honor an English soldier can earn). He was Sergeant major in the rifle brigade and besides being in the Crimea he was in the whole of the Indian war from the massacre at Cawnpore to the end of the mutiny. I can assure you he is about the best soldier in the whole Company. I find one fact worthy of mention, that is Englishmen are kinder, more straightforward and more manly in appearance and character than any other people I meet. There are three Englishmen in our tent. I think there are about 20 in the whole Company (one fifth) and yet though they are in such small proportion, every sergeant is an Englishman except the Quartermaster Sergeant whose duty it is to provide food and clothes for the men, and he is a rogue. Yesterday we had to remove to another part of the camp. It was pretty heavy work to carry all our tents and bunks etc. By and By we shall go into the wooden barracks which are in course of erection for us.

When the horses were taken to water yesterday I was busy and my pair were left behind, so I had to start about ten minutes after the rest. I had nothing but a night halter on each horse but they are very obedient and went off at a nice canter. I watered them and then set off back but had not got far before I met the officer of the day (a captain appointed to command the whole camp for 24 hours). He stopped me and asked my name and which battery I belonged to. He then told me to report myself to Cap. Warren under arrest for galloping my horses to water. I told him I had no bridle and they were too spirited to hold back. So he told me I had better get off and lead them. I did so of course, glad to get off so easily.

Byron is getting to walk round again and purposes to see Stanton, Sec. of War, about his commission very soon. He is or appears to be quite sure of getting it and also of getting a commission or some appointment for me, which will cause me to be transferred from this company. If I get a lieutenancy I can resign when I please.

We have got some new recruits this week. One of them was a *lawyer* in New York. He fully expected to be made a sergeant right away but instead of that he has been put into our detachment as driver. He is quite a dashy kind of fellow, very liberal with his cigars etc. He gave the Captain a box of cigars that cost him 5 dollars.

Our Sergeant who knew him in New York went to him and said, "Mr Moore, you are put in my detachment."

"Very good," said the lawyer. "Pray, in what capacity?"

"As Driver," said the sergeant.

"Driver! What? Driver!!! Impossible. Would you murder me in

cold blood? I never mounted a horse in my life, and safe as I do so I shall break my precious neck. Look at my hands. Do you think they look fit to clean your bloody horses? By Heavens, No. It cannot be. I must have a *position*. A position, sergeant."

"So you will have. A very high one, right on top of a big sorrel horse. All for the good of your country, Mr Moore," said the Sergeant laughing.

After a little musing the lawyer said, "Well! If so, so it is and so it stands. So. So . . . When I am an old man with grandchildren surrounding me I can tell them what I suffered in the days of the rebellion for the preservation of the Union. Ah, well, take a weed. Of course you will show me the ropes, won't you sergeant."

"Oh certainly, I will show you all I can."

"Let's Liquor!!"

Nov 8th. The Quartermaster Sergeant has been reduced to the ranks today by the Colonel and an Englishman named Maxwell has been put in his place.

It is very cool today but dusty and dry. I don't think it has rained for a fortnight. There is a surprising difference in the weather of this place and the p—pot of England. November in England is awfully wet and gloomy. But of course, I am now in the latitude of Sicily or thereabouts. The nights are just beginning to be frosty but I am told that winter only commences about the end of December and is severest in January and February.

I have a talk with Byron every day about something or other. He passes himself as an Englishman though of course he has told me different, and his accent is unmistakably foreign. If what he has told me be true, and I have not the slightest reason to doubt it, his life would be one of the most interesting ever written. When Major in the East India Company's service he was sent to Persia where he commanded the whole of the Persian army in two campaigns against the Afghans (I think). He wrote an account of these campaigns which appeared in an English periodical called the *Military Journal* or some such name. On his return he was made F.R.G.S. on account of some maps and explorations he made in the neighbourhood of Lake Coromain.

But the remarkable persons he has been connected with beats

44

everything. He has been privately presented to the Queen and Prince Albert, has been intimate with Charles Dickens and other English authors, and I might go on with many other surprising facts. Surprising because Byron is now a mere Corporal in the Army of the U.S.

Nov 10th. Yesterday we got a month's pay. I have spent 30 dollars since I came here, but as I have now nearly everything I want to make me comfortable, I shall be able to be more economical.

On Sunday we had Service in one of the Barracks in course of preparation. It was conducted by a Methodist minister from Washington. The Methodists are the strongest denomination in the States, but the congregation on Sunday was small. I am afraid there is not much religion of any kind amongst soldiers.

Our camp is situated about a mile from the Capitol, N.E. from Washington. The little Potomac is in view in one direction and the Dome of the Capitol in the other. The Baltimore road runs along one side of the camp and we are surrounded with woods on the other three sides. The Stars and Stripes waves over the centre of the camp just opposite the headquarters or tents of the Colonel and Adjutant. There are about 160 guards posted in various parts of the camp night and day or at least, that number is on guard but only one third is on duty at a time. No one can pass through the camp at night without knowing the countersign.

I am sorry I have not yet received any newspapers from you. You must not send any more. They get stolen by the Yankees before they get to me. Tell me if you have received any papers from me.

Nov 11th. We have had a hard day's drill today. The bugle sounded about 6 o'clock this morning for all the men to rise. Five minutes after the names were called and then we had half an hour for breakfast. Then went to the stables, cleaned the horses and fed them. This and cleaning the stables took till 8 o'clock. We then harnessed the horses and got ready for going out to drill. The drill ground is about a mile from here. It was after 11 when we got back. We had then to unharness the horses and take them to water and then feed them. It was now 12 o'clock.

At one we harnessed up again and drilled till after three. Then

45

watered, cleaned and fed the horses again, which took till ½ past 4 o'clock. Then we had tea and then the bugle sounded for retreat, which means that work is over for the day. The names were called and now it is 6 o'clock and I intend to finish this letter to post it in the morning.

Byron intends to go to see Stanton tomorrow. I feel doubtful of the result as I am afraid Stanton will think that Byron is too old for service as indeed he is. When I write again which will be immediately on the receipt of the answer to my last letter, I shall be able to tell you how he succeeded.

I sometimes wonder, but not very often, what people had to say about me when it was known that I was one of the missing at Farnworth. Did Deardens chuckle? Did people make curious guesses as to my place of refuge?

"Misther Duffy", the dacent man who would not have his wh—e of a daughter disgraced on account of her supreme innocence, by giving evidence for me. Asch!!! I feel sick with disgust when I speak of such an Irish bullfrog. What a catch he has made in that dried up specimen of the Feminine Gender with the specs and the cheek bones. And what an extraordinary catch she has made in such a sack full of m—, with ten little sacks to back him. *Vermin.*

When I come back which I believe I shall, I intend to have money enough to completely set at nought (I won't put the word defiance) the whole herd of fools and knaves, who are enemies to the *royal family* of the Horroxes.

Just as I am writing there is a violent controversy between the Englishmen and Yankees in our Tent as to the capabilities of this government of making war with France or England. Johnny Bull's representatives tells the Yankees they are unable to lick the South. This incontestible fact knocks all the other arguments into a roostered chapeau. (This is good Yankee now for Cocked hat.)

It is the general opinion here Lincoln will be re-elected President. Many of the papers express the same opinion. I think myself that the Confederate cause (perhaps I should say Rebel cause but I won't) is in a very unpromising condition.

Their great disadvantages are want of supplies and want of men before which any army must at last surrender. I don't think this war will last long anyway. What do you think?

Well I must now conclude. I think I have about exhausted my

stock of information. I am perfectly well in health as I most sincerely hope all at home can say. With best love I remain, Yours always,

James A. Horrocks

Write a long letter.

Camp Barry
Washington D.C.

Nov 20th. There are several changes being made today in the Company. Our Sergeant Hartell, and Dunning, the orderly Sergeant, have both resigned their stripes in consequence of a disagreeing with the Captain. Two newly enlisted men who have been in the regular army are to take their places.

Poor Old Byron is quite feeble and lame from the rheumatism. I wonder he does not write to get a commission if he has as much influence as he says he has, but he says he wants to see Stanton personally. I am afraid he will not be able again to get his old position because he is now too far past the meridian of life.

I don't know what to think of him scarcely. How is it that he has been in such an honorable position in this and in the British service and now only a corporal here. There may be circumstances that would bring about such a change but I think there must be a screw loose somewhere about him. Accident or misfortune is not sufficient reason to satisfy my mind. There is some grand blunder or other on his part. Perhaps he has disgraced himself someway. I don't know. But there is one fact which cannot be denied. That is if he is so long unable to get himself a commission it is scarcely possible that I have much to expect from him.

Well I am very well treated here. I have nothing to complain of. Good food, meat (salt or fresh twice a day), good clothing and comfortable lodging and yet I cannot help but feel that my talents might be better employed. But I will not complain or whine about outrageous fortune or my own mismanagement but feeling thankful that things are no worse I will make the best of the state into which the fates decided for me to come and remember, Bro. Joseph, "Derjenige welcher zufrieden ist, ist reich."

Our Captain is frightfully incompetent. He shows it every day. I am a better man that he is any end up. I can wop him if necessary. I

am better educated and I know already more of Artillery man-
oeuvres than he does.

*Nov 16th.** There are 16 men detailed out of our battery for guard
every day. It comes to my turn about once in five days. Out of the
whole 160 guards of the camp there are four chosen out of the ranks
by the adjutant to wait upon the Colonel.

They are called orderlies and are chosen according to their
appearance when inspected, the neatest, cleanest looking men with
the brightest sabres, buttons and epaulets. On Tuesday I was on
Guard and the adjutant picked me out as orderly. It is not only
considered an honor but a pass is given to each of the four for the
whole of the next day till 12 o'clock midnight. My duty was to
remain near the Colonel's tent and be ready for any duty which
might be required of me.

I spent most of the time in the Colonel's cook's tent. He is a
contraband—that is, an escaped slave. He escaped from his master
in Prince Georgia (a county of Maryland about 15 miles from here)
with his wife and children.

I was quite interested in him and could not help thinking of Uncle
Tom. I suppose he is a good specimen of his class. He is a Methodist
and has a good many texts of scripture by heart as well as hymns.
Amongst other things he told me he did not like to be called a nigger
because he is not a nigger. He says there is only one nigger and that
is the devil and he is a white man but was turned black for his
wickedness.

This old negro told me a good deal of his life which I dare say
would not be very interesting from my version. He is very good
natured, roasted some apples for me and gave me a roll of tobacco,
pure unadulterated leaf from the plantation of his old master. There
is an immense number of blacks round here. Nearly all the officers'
servants are black. They are generally first rate equestrians. One
little fellow in particular in the service of the Captain of the 19th
N.Y. will mount the big horse of his master and ride him to water. He
does not seem to care how the horse prances or gallops although he
is only like a little black doll on horseback. He sticks on like a brick.

This little fellow came up to the cook's tent when I was there on a
visit to the little black son of Uncle Tom. He came in grinning and
said to the cook's boy, "Brown, will you have an apple?" Brown

---

* *Sic*. He may mean *Nov 26th*.

took it and thanked him. By and By he said, "Brown will you have some cakes?" and gave him three gingerbread cakes. Then says, "Brown, will you have another apple?" and gave him another. All the time he himself was eating cakes and apples most voraciously from what appeared to be an inexhaustible store in his pocket. In answer to my questions he said he had formerly belonged to a planter in Norfolk. Never had a father or mother, sister, brother or any other relation. Does not know how old he is. (He seems to be about 10 but small for his age.) When the soldiers passed through Norfolk he followed them and has been with them since. Their battery was paid on the day I was speaking to him and he got plenty of money from the soldiers and officers, *all* of which he makes a point of spending on his own pleasure as he says he has no one to take care of his money and does not want anyone else to have any benefit from it when he is dead. I think this must be Topsy's brother.

How far do you think this place is from slavedom? Just about 3 miles. Maryland and Virginia (parts of which are in sight from here) are both slave states. The District of Columbia is free but if any slaves escape to here and their master says he is a Union man, he can be taken back.

On Thursday I got a pass from the Colonel for the whole day till 12 o'clock midnight but did not set out for Washington till after dinner. I enjoyed myself pretty well. No intoxicating liquor is allowed to be sold to soldiers here. Not even a glass of beer. Everything is very dear in Washington. Just for a good tea, including a pork steak and fried potatoes, I paid 60 cents. For having my hair cut 25 cents and for a shave 10 cents. I bought a comforter for a dollar and a pair of gloves for a dollar and a quarter.

Poor old Byron is worse and has now been taken to the hospital.

Yesterday there was a grand review of the Artillery in this camp. There was blank cartridge shot and one poor fellow had his hand blown off. There is considerable danger in learning artillery drill. No battery ever learns the drill without a few being killed or crippled, so it is said. One of our Company is lame. His horse got entangled in the traces when giving the countermarch on a gallop and fell with the poor fellow's leg under him. It was only through the other drivers halting quickly that his life was saved.

I have been kicked twice by the horses, not by my own though. I was riding to water about 10 days since and the off horse of a team just passing threw up its heels and struck my left leg but with no serious result, only a black place. The other time I was grooming a pair of horses for another fellow and the one I was cleaning was bit by the other and tried to kick back, but as I was just cleaning his fetlocks behind I came in for a push which sent me on my beam ends. When you remember that I once run "Owd Hossky's keaws" till they gave no milk that day, you will not be surprised when I tell you that I took my whip and thrashed both horses till they sweat and then finished my work without further interruption.

Dec 4th. I have received your letter today and am especially pleased with the accounts of your, or I ought to say our, pecuniary prosperity. There is one thing which is a question with me, whether it will pay you better to invest your money in building a house in Edgeworth, or to let someone else build it and employ the money in the waste trade. I have also received the *Bolton Chronicle* which I have been reading with much interest. From one portion which refers to the Clerkship of the Board of Guardians I see that G.T.D. is still on the loose and offers his valuable services for 25s. a week although of course he can make 3 £ a week very easily as a butter merchant. (One small keg a week with me for a partner. Oh what a humiliating retrospection.)

Dec 6th. I was interrupted when I got thus far with my letter and have not been able to resume my pen till just now. It is Sunday. Yesterday I got another *Chronicle*, which is the same date as the other, and the *Illustrated London News* but not *Punch*. If you sent it it has been prigged.

It was reported that our battery was to be sent to Buffalo to be ready for an invasion of the rebels living in Canada. But it proved a hoax. Our battery is not competent enough to be sent anywhere yet.

Your description of that Saturday night when William brought his fiddle to have a little jubilee in Devonport house made me heartily wish I could have shared the fun and shoved my nose in proximity to the foam on the surface of those chips and shavings which Walter brought out of the cellar in a quart pot.

It would do you good to see our battery at drill. Everything is done in obedience to the sound of the bugle. I drive the lead team of the second section, the most responsible place in the whole battery, but I have a good ear for music and never mistake the bugle sound. I think sometimes that my horses have learnt some of the bugle sounds, they need so little guiding.

I am intending to go to Washington next week and shall try to hear a debate in Congress, as the session commences on the 8th of this month.

I am in good health as I hope you are all of you. I cannot think of anything to add to this epistle so I will simply subscribe myself as ever,

Your most affectionate son with oceans of love
James A. Horrocks

What a devil of a name. I wish I had my own name. I might get a little influence perhaps from the gentlemen in New York.

Corporal Peters says he can send this letter to England to be posted in Liverpool. I will try him.

5th N.J. Battery
Camp Barry
Washington
Dec 25th '63

My Dear Dad,
I received your letter dated Nov 30th 1863, yesterday. You *can* write a *first-rate letter*, there's no mistake about it. To say I enjoyed the reading of it only conveys the faintest idea of the real delight with which my eyes travelled along the lines of your old familiar handwriting. Your descriptions are graphic and amusing—but the best part of the matter is that you are all *well* and *happy* and I know it will not lessen your enjoyment to know that I am also well and my heart was never lighter or more inclined for mirth than on this beautiful Christmas day. Although Christmas will be past and the New Year 1864 will be well begun when you receive this, I must tell you that at the present moment while I am writing this I sincerely wish you

A MERRY CHRISTMAS AND A HAPPY NEW YEAR
and many more to come with me with you to be happy altogether.

I expect Bro. Joseph will be the entire manager of the Lancashire & Yorkshire Railway Co. yet. Tell him I know *he will win*, and also tell him that his Bro. Jamie will come in by no means the last horse, that is if he gets anything like a fair chance in the race. As for Bro. William he has won already and to express his various excellencies in as few words as possible, I will use the elegant phrase of a friend of mine to whom I lent my *blacking brush*—You are a *gentleman*, and a *scholar* and a good judge of *human nature*, and *whiskey toddy*.

As for Bro. Harry, he is one of Nature's Volcanoes, overflowing with the milk of human kindness and good humour. And I agree with you that he would produce a sensation. His imaginary conflict with John C. Heenan would bring down the house if he went on the stage. And then to produce a *serio-comic* effect he would only need to give the recitation describing the return of the young man home to his parents and sweetheart from America and I bet five cents to a pumpkin, the audience would both *laugh and cry*. And Miss Mort is the handsomest girl in Farnworth today.

My Dear Dad—You say, Did te ever yer sitch a tale i thi life, as thy Mother axing for £5 0s. 0d.? Well I have heard many a tale of the same sort. I agree with you it is *impudence* but at the same time it *is nothing* to compare with *your own modest self-assurance* in asking for the small profit of 6d per lb. on cotton waste. Well after all it was only *shent per shent* and it is not likely you would give any credit for such small profit. I *wouldn't*. Make em pay cash down. Keep the wheel agoing.

Reading your description of that Saturday night supper when Bro. Joseph read my letter, made me feel as if I should have very much enjoyed that evening at home, and gone down to the bottom of those *orkard* steps to bring a *pot full* up. The character you gave the bread was good but we have had that *very best bread* so often that it won't do you know. You can't impose on me.

You are just a *leetle* too transparent for this precocious child.

I have received a Christmas present from a young lady in Elmira in the west of New York State. Don't be alarmed—I am not. The way it came about is rather curious. One of the decentest boys in the Company, named Jackson, got me to write letters for him when we were at Trenton both to his wife and parents. And as his wife came to see him from Elmira before we left for Washington, I was introduced to her and she begged I would let her have one of my photographs when I got some taken. I promised to do so and kept my promise. A cousin of Mrs Jackson—Miss Annie Strachen—saw and admired my shadow and sent a message by Mrs Jackson's letter for me to let her have one of my photographs too. To this I offered no objection and made as polite a reply as possible as Jackson assured me that the young lady was rich and well brought up and her age is sweet nineteen. I have received her Carte de Visite in return for mine, and now Jackson has received a box from his wife in Elmira full of all sorts of nice things, and a message from his wife to say that he must share the eatables with his friend Ross. (I know him well.) These eatables consist of roasted chickens, plum cake, tea, sugar, big lump of fresh butter, sweet cakes, apples, nuts etc. But in addition there was a parcel set apart for my especial benefit from the said Miss Annie.

When I opened it I found a *plum pudding* ornamented round the top with wax flowers, and also a small case apparently made by the very kind young lady containing thread, pins and needles, and buttons, all arranged in the neatest possible style. We have kept all these things till today when Jackson and I intended to have a regular blow out *regardless of expense* but we have determined to defer it another day in consequence of a most delightful circumstance which was unexpected.

The whole Company are about to have a blow out at the expense of the Company fund which is raised by what provisions we have in excess of the actual wants of the company. The first part of the blow out I received just before commencing this letter—about a nuggin of whiskey punch. The second part will come in about an hour from now, at 1 o'clock. Just wait and I will tell you what we got for dinner.

Dec 26. We got roast turkey and plum pudding. The dining room was ornamented with festoons of evergreen so that it really looked and *felt* like Christmas.

I have been over to Lincoln hospital (about 20 minutes walk from here) today to see our old friend, Byron. He was very glàd to see me. His face actually beamed with pleasure as he shook me with both hands. He walks about and seems much better than before. He says he has written to a friend of his, a Colonel who is raising an Ambulance Corps in New York, to get me a *lieutenancy* and says he is certain that the said Colonel is such an old friend of his that he will be sure to oblige him. I should certainly be delighted to get out of this into such a better position. The Ambulance Corps is a Cavalry

Company which does no fighting but merely directs and guards the immense trains of Ambulance waggons moving from place to place in connection with the army and consequently I should stand a rather better chance of coming *whum to my mother* with all my legs and arms complete, and in addition to that it would be a more fitting and proper thing to be lieutenant Horrocks than private *Ross*.

In this land of freedom and liberty—Hail, Columbia!!!—I have always thought there was a very frequent use made of bowie knives and revolvers. This was before I came here. And now I can testify to the fact. As our Holland School acquaintance said—I *always thought so* and now *I am sure of it*. I have seen plenty of fighting and have seen bowie knives drawn in a fight, but murder has always been prevented by the bystanders in every case I have been witness to. There are some of the worst characters in the army that heaven ever permitted to breathe and some Companies have the felicity to possess more of these *rowdies* than others.

Our Company is fortunately one of the most respectable class. But there is a regiment of Cavalry stationed near this camp— *Baker's Cavalry*—that seems to be composed of lawless men. About a month ago a fight took place between a party of them and a party of Artillery men. It began in a quarrel between one of each party in a lager bier saloon and ended in a general mêlée in the road.

A detachment of the guard in this camp went with sabres and revolvers and put a stop to it, but not before two artillerymen were killed and about seven wounded, one of the Cavalry killed and several wounded. Since then there have been several smaller quarrels and fights, and now it is unsafe for anyone to be alone on the road to Washington from here at night. Last Monday two of our men were carried into the barracks senseless. One of them died without speaking a word in two hours and a half and the other one can walk about now with plasters on his head.

It turns out that they were met by six of Baker's Cavalry and asked for their money. This they refused to give up and they were both at once knocked down and kicked and beaten mercilessly. A lieutenant happened to be coming along on horseback and he at once set spurs to his horse and galloped up. The cowardly six turned tail and ran but he kept them in sight and succeeded in at length having them all six lodged in custody and then came back and had the two unlucky ones carried to their barracks which was known by the cross cannons and the figure 5 on their caps. These six *highwaymen* will be tried by court martial and it is to be hoped will meet the penalty they richly deserve by dancing a hornpipe in the empty air to the tune of Jack Ketch. Last Wednesday there was a grand Review took place by General Barry and some of the members of Congress of all the Artillery in our Camp and in Camp Marshall not far from here. We were reviewed on a large plain near Lincoln Hospital. All the batteries were arranged in rank and the General passed along the front with his *Suite*. After that each battery made a left wheel and walked— Order in Column—past the grandstand over which floated the *Star Spangled Banner*.

When every battery had passed and were again in their old positions, a fat country looking gentleman—Representative of some place in Ohio—was heard to say to the general, "Now General they have walked past very nicely—Just give us something lively— Make them run like *the very devil*." So the General gave the order to Double Quick!!! And then the earth fairly shook under the tramp of more than 1500 horses and the rolling of so many pieces. It was *splendid* and *exciting*. With whip and spur I was the lead driver of our battery, and when nearly to the grandstand passed a caisson of the 33rd N.Y. which was literally smashed by a collision with one of the pieces. The cannoneers who were unhurt were standing near and the drivers, dismounted, were holding their horses. When I saw the wreck, I could not help giving a *fiendish yell*, which must have given the horrors to the lady spectators round the general. . . . After this we returned home. The casualties, not reckoned in destruction of property, were happily all included in the items of one broken leg and one horse killed.

We have received news this week of the fight between the celebrated Benicia Boy and Tom King, and I cannot help feeling a little satisfaction to know that poor John C. H. came off second best. Some of the more bigoted and conceited Yankees had the impudence to say that their countryman had not had fair play, but they knew better in their hearts and Heenan will be at a discount after this.

We are now living in barracks in which it is much warmer and more comfortable. We have a dining room and have more convenience for cleanliness and comfort than in tents.

I have posted two Illustrated papers for you about a week since.
I thought you had kept my destination secret—but it appears it is
well known in Farnworth. Well that is no matter. But I should not
like you to show my photograph to anyone as they would see at
once I had got a uniform of some kind on and would naturally guess
that I was a soldier, which I should not like anyone to know unless I
was an *officer*. I am glad Bro. William intends to write me a long
letter. I will send one of my photographs in this letter for him. I
ought to have had my spurs on and epaulets and belt with sabre and
revolver, to look like an artilleryman in full dress.

I am surprised to hear that Mrs Wilson should have defended me
when speaking to the new preacher as I thought she would have
been one to give scandal its full force and benefit. But of course I am
no less pleased than surprised.

I fully approve of your resolution to get as much money as
possible in as little time as possible.

It is very probable that the pay of the officers and soldiers will be
considerably increased soon. If I get the lieutenancy I so ardently
wish for, I shall have about 105 dollars a month at the present rate of
payment.

I hope Walter will get a prize for drawing and also shall be glad to
know that Peter and Benjamin are getting on well. You do not say
anything about George in your letter. I have not mentioned Sister
Annie in this letter but I must not forget her. Give her my best love,
and accept the same yourself and all the family.

I want some photographs.

Your loving son
James

Washington D.C.
Jany 1st 1864

My Very Dear Bro. William,
Your welcome letter came to hand yesterday, the last day in the
old year. I was very much gratified to hear of your abundant success.
With regard to your idea of having me for your assistant, I assure
you that such an occupation would suit me exactly and I think I
should become the most expert and useful assistant that ever a son

of Esculpius had the happiness to possess. But the idea though pleasing is unfortunately impracticable. There is not only a few yards of *ocean brines* between us but there is also a chain which seems likely to bind me here for something like 2 years-and-a-half longer, and besides that there is an obstacle in the way of my returning in the shape of a *fine boy* whose grandmother would be too glad to see me and say like Macbeth to the dagger, "Let me clutch thee." Well you know I am a sort of determined youth and I would much rather stay in this country and carve a fortune for myself than come home, happy and comfortable as it is, like a cur with its tail between its legs and become deservedly the laughing stock of the various babboons, raccoons and Spanish donkeys whom I renounce now and for ever.

I think it would have been better for me if I had waited patiently and got a mercantile situation in New York instead of coming here but after all there are more chances in war for an Adventurer like myself than there can be anywhere else. As for getting killed, do not imagine I am such a soft noodle as to be frightened. There is only about one chance in twenty that I get shot and I shall take care to make the chances still smaller if I see any danger. If I am not successful in getting a commission and our battery gets into action, I think I will purposely get taken prisoner and then it will not be difficult to get paroled and I can then do as I think proper only of course not to enter the Union army again.

I think I shall win my way yet by some means or other. I have no encumbrance, and though I say it myself have no mean abilities and besides that I have a determination which will surmount many difficulties. Therefore if Providence will only smile upon me I shall come home yet and have plenty of beefsteaks and onions and good *Yale*, and plenty of fiddle and piano and many a good laugh out of my funny old dad, our loving, rosy faced, benevolent, old dad. I find you did not *pat*ronize *Pat*'s wedding. I am glad of it. Your presence ought to grace more aristocratic and less empty society than that of the fawning hypocritical Dogs.

You do right to ride first class and thank goodness you are likely to be able to continue to ride first class as long as you live.

The place where your new house is to be built is well chosen. I recognised the locality at once from your sketch which was not bad by any means. Have you begun to build, or are you only thinking of beginning? I suppose you will borrow the money. Who will you borrow it from?

I enclosed my Carte de Visite for you in a letter which I posted for home on Monday last, and shall be very glad indeed to receive yours and also Joseph's and Henry's separately.

I am spending this New Year's Day in a different manner and in much different society than I should were I in Lancashire. After the "reveille", or the call to rise from our beds, I breakfasted on bread, coffee and salt pork. Then marched down to the stable and rode down to the watering place with the horses. On returning to the stable, I fed and groomed my pair, which this morning was no easy matter as the ground is knee deep in mud. But I have nothing more to do till three o'clock except to have my dinner, which will consist of boiled beef, vegetable soup and bread.

At three o'clock the horses must be looked after in the same way as this morning and at half past four we return to the barracks and get ready for dress parade, which implies polishing boots and brightening up your buttons and epaulets, washing yourself and brushing your clothes. Dress parade is perhaps the gayest sight in the whole camp. The entire body of men in their best clothes and in their cleanest turn-out are arranged on a square in the front of the Colonel's headquarters called the parade ground. They are arranged along three sides of the square and at the command from the adjutant we present sabres to the Colonel who stands in front about the centre of the square. He politely lifts his hat and tells the adjutant to read the general orders. This is done and in case a court martial has been held in the camp, the sentences are read, and after a quick march has been played by the buglers the parade is dismissed. We return to barracks, have supper (bread and tea) with dried apples (stewed perhaps) and then spend the evening as we please till ½ past 8 o.c. when the men are turned out for roll call, and at 9 o'clock "Taps", or the bugle call for lights out and go to sleep, is sounded. All this is very different you will admit from the manner I formerly spent New Year's Day, but still it might be very much worse. The United States govt., or as the soldiers say "Uncle Sam" is very good to the men who fight for him.

You say that Memory is a pleasing faculty to you. So it is to me and I believe to everyone whose consciences are unburdened with crime. I shall not soon forget the walks I had with you in the neighbourhood of Edgeworth. One Sunday we went over Turton heights and when we got to the top the wind was so strong that we pretended to make sails with our arms and tacked about like a ship. The scenery in Edgeworth is pleasant in some places, but my dear fellow, you have not seen *American scenery*. I should dearly like to transpose you instantly to this bunk of mine in the barracks, and then take you for a walk along the Baltimore road. We should meet real *Yankees* on the road. Don't look surprised. Next we might meet some darkies, men or women, with baskets on their arms or driving light waggons. Then we come to a bridge leading over a river, a tributary of the Potomac, but here a man with a musket and shining buttons on a blue coat would demand my *pass*. This I would show him and pass on. On the other side of the river the ground rises rather suddenly and when we have ascended a certain distance we come to a fort of stone and dirt armed with Parrott guns. I know one of the soldiers here belonging of course to a battery of heavy Artillery, and for that reason we could go into the fort and inspect the whole afair. When we got here I would tell you to turn round and look at the city of Washington, as you can see the city with more advantage from here than from any other point I believe. The Capitol is the most conspicuous object. The city seems very irregular and straggling. The Post Office and the obelisk of General Washington, now in course of erection, are also prominent objects. It is useless to try and describe everything we should see. One thing I ought to mention, that is Every black woman bows to a soldier and every negro takes off his hat. But the great feature of this part of the country that would strike any stranger is its extremely military character. In the walk I have just described we should see at least half a dozen camps and as many forts, besides passing a government corral which is capable of accommodating about 15,000 horses, though there is not that number at present in it.

Jany 2nd. It is Saturday today. There is no drill. The night has been extremely cold, and in place of the mud of yesterday, the ground is hard and from the previous impressions of horses and men and waggon wheels is very rough. Today we are sending away the dead body of our "Guidon" or flag bearer. He is a mere boy of seventeen and the only son of his mother who is a widow. He would have been buried here with military honors but his mother wished to have him buried in the old cemetery at home. He was a general favorite and his death which was sudden was caused by typhoid fever. It caused quite a gloom to be over the battery. I can not help thinking of an American song of which this is a part:

> Farewell sweet Mother
> Every night I've dreamed of thee,
> And thy voice was kind and gentle
> Saying pleasant things to me.
> While you these vigils keep,
> Now I lay me down to sleep.
> Mother tell me why you weep.
> Oh! weep not now for me.
> Farewell—sweet mother.
> Weep not mother now for me.

Corporal Peters received a telegram from New York that his child was dead. He was in great distress about it and received a furlough for a week. He had not money to pay his fare home and I lent him 11 dollars. He has not returned though his furlough expired on Christmas day and has now been reported a deserter. I can not but believe that he will pay me back the money, as he was such a thoroughly honest and good natured fellow, but time will show. If he does not send it to me I shall cease to put faith in anyone.

I should like to see a plan of your house. Just a rough one with a sketch of the front part. Never mind your backside.

Old Byron has not yet received a reply from the Colonel to whom he wrote on my behalf. I suppose it is very foolish on my part ever to have expected that he should. . . . I am as right as a clock. Oh, I say old boy—We shall have some lots of things to talk about when we see one another again.

> Old England for ever.
> No power shall sever
> My heart from the land of my birth.
> 'Tis the land of the free. So it ever shall be.
> 'Tis the happiest land upon earth.

Your most affectionate Bro.
James

Camp Barry
Washington D.C.
Jany 17th 1864

My Dear Father and Mother,

I had begun to fear that the letter posted, or sent to be posted in Liverpool, had by some means miscarried and was therefore very much pleased to get yours of the 26th ult. yesterday. And now being Sunday and inspection being over, I have an opportunity to answer you.

I am glad that Annie, Walter and Peter were pleased with their letters and the reason I did not write one to Benjamin is because he did not write one to me. And he is quite big enough, you must all admit.

You advise me to ask the proper authorities for promotion and prove to them the promise made by Captain Warren. Now the only authority to promote me—besides those very high up—is Captain Warren. He has again made me Clerk to the Company, so that I cannot even make a complaint that would be taken notice of. I even doubt whether any notice would be taken of it if I was not Clerk. They are paying high prices for Volunteers and do not like to lose any of them. They have lost a good many out of our battery and the Captain has gone to the state of New Jersey to recruit again. In consequence of our want of men I am still in charge of my horses, but when the Captain returns with more men I shall have only to assist Maxwell, the Quartermaster Sergeant. He has been doing the work himself for a long time but now as there is some chance of him getting a lieutenancy, it is necessary that someone should learn how to keep the accounts.

There is one more good hope of a commission—There are wanted something like two thousand officers for *coloured troops*, and there are examinations now being made in Washington of soldiers and civilians who feel competent to try. The only thing I am required to know that at present I feel unable to compete for a commission is—*infantry tactics* but this I can get up in the course of a month or six weeks and then I will get a recommendation from Capt. Warren and *go in and win*. . . . As for coming home, I assure you I am far happier here than I should be if that miserable old hag gained her ends.

You are such a good soul that I believe you would be willing to pay the money and have me home again than not. You say I should have nothing to fear. Now I think I *should have* a good deal to annoy me if I came home, and paying would be the greatest annoyance of all. . . . But on the other hand I am as unwilling as you are to waste three years of the best part of my life in such a service as this, and perhaps get killed into the bargain and I shall therefore take certain steps, if I fail in getting a lieutenancy. I have not yet determined what will be the best but shall be governed by circumstances in great measure. However I think that I could get to New York any time I like in spite of all the detectives and Yankee devils that exist, and from New York could ship for Liverpool or London. I think to the latter. There I could get a situation of some kind—I am not as particular as I was once.

If I got a place as a porter, I might prove myself honest and steady and show that I could write my name, and do a *simple sum in addition* and then become clerk, and could pay you a visit without fear of being arrested by the enemy.

Oh shouldn't I like to have one jolly night at home—Eh, wor? Couldn't I entertain you half an hour—Perhaps not. But I would make a bet of greenback to a goolden suv'rin, if anybody liked to take me up on it—that I could just manage to amuse, instruct, edify, and entertain you for *above* 30 minutes. Don't you believe me? Yes my Golly I know I could. But I am not homesick. I am 20 years of age and a *soldier* and it would not be exactly the thing to say I was crying for my *mammy*.

But I should like to see her and all of you, as well as those beefsteaks, curran' cakes, mawfins and that quart pot with a snip out of the edge with round shoulders. I can see these things while I am writing as well as the kitchen dresser and that rocking chair which I got into every time my dad got up to drink. This was not as seldom as President Lincoln might suppose.

We have had service in the barracks this afternoon, on account of the death of the other man who was beaten by the cavalry. You may remember the circumstances I mentioned in the last letter I sent you. This man partially recovered from the effects of his hammering but has had a turn for the worse and poor fellow is now dead. He spoke a funny mixture of the Lancashire dialect and Yankee slang. I once asked him if he knew how far it was from Wernuth to 't Mump. "Ay—Aw guess I do—By gum. Yes, sirree Bob. Awve bin to

Owdham." I do not know what has been done to the six ruffians who killed him. Very likely *nothing*. Such things are of frequent occurrence.

I rejoice to hear of Bro. Joseph's success and wish it still more abundant.

Your kindness to Haas was a mark of your affection to myself. I appreciate it. And although he could not come, he must have appreciated it too. He is a *sponger* as Bro. Joseph says, but he was and is still *very fond of me*, so I believe. He begins his letter,

Dear, Dear Horrocks,
    Absence makes the heart grow fonder.—Ah! had I known your address, *months* should not have elapsed without some communication at least on my part. I at least have often, very often remembered you and now Horrocks I have done with Westminster etc.

He then gives a short account of the year's course at Westminster, crowning the whole report by this expressive sentence, "Old Boy, do you remember last year, eh? What a Spree!!! Eh, this has been quite a different time I can assure you. No sprees—all *solemn hypocrisy*."

This letter was very entertaining you may be sure and I think I must send him a reply. But shall not tell him that I am a soldier but keep up the delusion of Clerk to a travelling gentleman.

I do not think there need be any alarm about Bro. George's silence. A sailing ship meets with many checks and delays in such a long voyage as that to the East Indies, and after he has reached Calcutta, it is a pretty long time before news of the ship's arrival can reach the owners in Liverpool. If he wrote a letter in Calcutta it might have miscarried even supposing that they have arrived there. Your first news of the ship's safe passage must be from the owners of the ship in Liverpool. Harrison is the name I think, is it not?

Those disasters at sea which you mention are very dreadful and heartrending but they are near the coast of Britain and not in the least likely to influence the ship *Labrador*.

Your account of the tea meeting at Farnworth day school gave me much satisfaction as it showed that you are still very much liked and very much respected in Farnworth.

Our William is not by profession a stump orator or a lecturer but I have no doubt he can and did make a good speech at the tea party and I am sure there was no family gave a better appearance or produced a better impression at that meeting than ours.

It is high time that our Henry should be more than a porter. I am very glad indeed that he is now High and Dry in the office, and sincerely should like to see him with an income big enough for a gentleman of his merit and necessities.

You describe Sister Annie as trimming bonnets for herself and mother. It will save considerable expense I should think. Annie is now nearly sixteen. She ought to be a *very accomplished young lady* now.

Jany 18. We have had snow on the ground ever since New Year's Day. But yesterday it began to thaw and today it has been raining heavily. In consequence of the slippery weather we took up all the horses to be shod at the government blacksmith's shop in Washington.

All the horses were shod in a very short time. A regiment of a thousand cavalry or artillery horses can be shod there in a few hours. This war is carried on in a gigantic style—and I do think the South must give way before such odds. But at the same time I do not wish *this child* to be one of the attacking party unless I am in command.

Jany 21st. I have been so busy making out the quarterly returns with Maxwell that I could not find time to finish this letter. I met with a man going up to the examination for a commission in coloured troops, yesterday. O'Brien introduced him to me. O'Brien asked him a few questions to test his general information. He asked him what was the principal Naval sea port of Russia. He answered *Cherbourg*. He did not know the difference between an obtuse angle and a right angle. Well thought I, if this man gets a commission, it is not *impossible* for me to obtain one too.

Well if I do well and good, $115 a month will keep me very comfortably. But if not, I shall look out for a chance and when I get a good one I will give Captain Warren the slip. But although I believe as I said before that I could reach New York in safety, yet at present I should run a risk of being caught and imprisoned, and a risk is not a thing to be desired if the operation can be made without any and I think it can.

Please excuse any more at present. I see it is not a very short letter even now and I cannot think of any other news to tell you. Hoping you are all well. Believe me with the most hearty love and affection for you all to be

Your own
Jamie

Sunday Jany 24th. I must send off this letter today. Three Batteries left our Camp this morning for New Orleans. We ought to have been payed above a week since but the payday is put off till March, and then I shall receive about 4 months' pay (my surplus clothing account will however be deducted 7½ dollars).
    J.H.

Camp Barry, D.C.
Feby 21st 1864

My Dear Parents,
    I am still in this Camp but how long I shall remain is very uncertain. It is expected that we shall receive marching orders very soon. My hopes of a commission are *gone*. The examination for commissions in coloured troops requires a very minute knowledge of Infantry tactics, which I have been entirely unable to prepare, owing to want of time, as my work as Company Clerk is very tedious and when I have a little leisure time I like to spend it in the open air better than studying Infantry tactics. Byron poor fellow is still in the hospital and I have given up all hopes of assistance from that quarter. If we were staying here long I believe I might get a commission in a Negro Regt. but unless I can have time to get the entire thing off by heart I shall stand no chance.
    I received your letter on the 14th with great joy and was much interested in its contents. Bro. George's safe arrival in Calcutta is very satisfactory and perhaps the next time you write you will be able to give him my address. I have pondered the matter over a very long time, very carefully and have come to the conclusion that when our Battery starts for the scene of action I shall start *for Philadelphia*. My plans are all laid and are too simple and carefully considered to fail. And even if they do fail, that is if I am arrested in the attempt, the only charge that can be brought against me will be

"Absence without leave", the punishment for which would be merely nominal. You must know that a soldier has to be absent 10 days before he can be considered a deserter. Again if I once went to the front with the Battery I would not attempt to leave before the expiration of the term as desertion from the front is often punished by death and I would rather risk my life in fighting than risk it by desertion. You do not need to fear for me in the least. Looking at the worst side of the question, that is if I get caught, the punishment will not be death. Well now I assure you I shall just go to Philadelphia without any danger. The plan I shall adopt is simply this. *Brady* will send my box to a place in Washington where I am acquainted. I shall go to this house and change my military garb for a suit of English clothes in the box, then go straight to the railway station and take a ticket for Philadelphia. If I am questioned by the detectives, I am an Englishman named J.H., have been on a visit to Washington to see the public buildings etc—if proof is wanted they may haul over my box and will find overwhelming proofs that I am what I say I am. And then in Philadelphia there is not the most remote chance of meeting anyone I know, and Philadelphia is a busy place where anyone may get a living. Another fortnight will probably see me out of this. Therefore do not write again until you hear from me and in all times of writing to me in the future let no mention or reference be made to this period of my *military* life. I am sure I shall be able to get employment in some shape very soon, and there will not be as much chance of my being arrested as there would be of finding a needle in a bottle of hay.

I am more than ever determined to give them the slip. *Maxwell*, the Quartermaster Sergeant, is about to be promoted to a lieutenancy. Now if the captain would only give the position to me (I am the fittest person for it) I would willingly stay with him and he would find me a faithful and competent person. But instead of that he is going to make *Steele* (fortunately an Englishman) into the Quartermaster Sergeant. Steele is an educated gentlemanly fellow and has hitherto been always employed at headquarters, i.e. keeping various regimental accounts for the colonel, and I cannot therefore very much grumble on account of his being promoted. But this only makes it still more unlikely that I can get to be Quartermaster Sergeant. He is a competent person and likely to keep it. I can keep my position as Company Clerk but whenever there is fighting I shall have to take part, as either cannoneer or driver. But if I am Quartermaster Sergeant I should take charge of the baggage waggons instead and I am therefore willing to stay in the Company if the Captain will promote me to that position. But if not, which is most probable, then I shall *skedaddle*. If I was in England or in the English service I should consider that it was a shame and a sin to desert but—you know the old adage—When you are in Rome do as the Romans do. When you are in Turkey do as the Turkeys do etc.

Well here I am in the land of Yankee doodle and I assure you that what would be considered in England and what I would consider myself as a disgraceful action is here regarded universally as a *Smart thing* and the person who does it is a *dem'd smart fellow*. Everyone tries to be *smart* and expect you to be *smart* too—if you have any gumption.

(This paper is too thin to write on both sides.)

Altogether, it just amounts to this. If I go out as *private* I may be *killed* and die without honor and glory—and more than that I shall die without being any benefit to you. If I am made Quartermaster Sergeant there is then a chance of a commission and a good prospect of returning safe and sound.

Feby 23. I thought we should get paid on the beginning of March but I am afraid the Captain thinks that it is more advisable to wait until after we have left here before we are paid, because he knows that there are very many in the Company who intend to desert when they get paid. (He does not suspect me in the least.) Fortunately I have money enough to answer my purposes without getting the pay now due to me.

I am as hearty as a buck, and am pleased to hear from your letter that you are all enjoying the same robust health, with the exception of my dear dad, whose tumble in the yard seems to have given no kind of sorrow to that heartless son of his—*Harry*—who instead of condoling with his venerable sire—*facetiously* remarks that he thought it was an earthquake. He ought to be downright well ashamed of himself. Talking about an earthquake puts me in mind of that Liverpool explosion you mentioned. I received your Newspaper and also the London *Punch*. Mr Barnes's speech is good.

Trade is indeed in a miserable state at Farnworth judging from what you say. I am sorry you cannot do anything more in the Waste trade, but there is no use repining. Things are sure to mend by and by. (I can not mention the date of improvement though.) I see from the papers that *War* has commenced between Denmark and the German powers. But I suppose it cannot be of very long duration if poor little Denmark receives no assistance and it seems that England's foreign policy is to be always neutral. Earl Derby does not agree with Earl Russell on that point but I think it is the best policy for England although perhaps not to be considered the most glorious and honorable.

I cannot tell, my dear Mother, how soon this war will be over, but the newspapers as usual talk about the great blow which it is intended shall be struck at the very heart of the Confederacy very shortly. But this is all stuff. Without any kind of exaggeration I believe the Rebels to be a match for the Yankees, as far as fighting goes, but the state of finances and provisions for the soldiers and people of the south are scant. It is a complicated question, and perplexes many wiser heads than mine. I am glad you did not tell Bro. George that I had enlisted for, as you say, he might let it out. This I do not wish to be the case. I do not want anyone to know. The explosion in Liverpool must have been a dreadful occurrence, but whatever accident happens, we shall always find, as in this case, that it might have been worse.

William is doing well. This is very pleasant. Suppose Father had brought up all his sons as factory operatives, made Joseph a *stripper and grinder* as Mr Barnes suggested, and Bro. William a *twister in* etc, where would he be now with his family? *Thank God* he displayed the judgement of a *wise man*.

You mention Miss Polly and Miss Tizzy Entwistle paying you a visit. This calls to mind a very pleasant day I spent in the "Jumbers" in the company of Miss Polly. John Wright of execrable memory was there the same day. He kept or assisted to keep the spirits of the whole company up to the boiling point.

In looking over some old letters I found one from Bro. Harry that was written to me when at College. Even now I laughed at some parts of it and wish he would write me one now. You say that Miss Mort is as hearty and handsome as ever. It gives me pleasure to hear it. I think she was the only one out of our own family at Farnworth who bade me goodbye. I cherish a most affectionate regard for her, and hope you will tell her that I sent my love to her (A brother's love you know). There is very little to add. I hope you will not blame me or think me rash and foolish in the step I am about to take, because such is not the case. I am cool, collected and long headed, can take care of myself, and therefore with very best love to you my dear parents, to my brothers and sisters, I remain most dutifully

Your own son.

Camp Barry D.C.
March 30th 1864

My Dear Parents,

You are most likely surprised at my long silence, and perhaps you will be more so when you see that this letter comes from Camp Barry, instead of from Philadelphia, as I gave you to understand in my last letter would be my residence by this time. Circumstances have however prevented me carrying out the plan I then proposed to myself. I also wished to see whether the Captain would favor me with regard to the position of Quartermaster Sergeant, which I said was about to become vacant, by the promotion of Maxwell. I have been patiently waiting for this event and as I *feared* the Captain has favoured the other clerk at Headquarters. I have now written to Brady for my box to be sent to a place in Washington, and therefore shall be most probably on my way to Philadelphia before long. The Captain as well as everybody else here, is much surprised that we have not yet received marching orders. All the ammunition is packed in the chests of the caissons or carriages, and all is ready for an order to come for the Battery to leave. But this is uncertain as to time and I should not be at all surprised if marching orders came tomorrow, or if we remained here another month. There is much dissatisfaction amongst the men on account of the long delayed payday. However I expect that we shall get two months' pay before long. But the Captain is afraid that, if they received all the pay due, many of them would not stay with him long. Consequently he is keeping them waiting till we leave here as he knows it will be more difficult to desert then. I received Bro. William's letter some days ago (dated March 1st) and read it with much pleasure, especially the part referring to his treatment of Mr Barlow's child with Dr Walker. I am sure he would have saved the child if it had been within the range of possibility.

The fact of M. J. Hamer's child being an Idiot ought I think to settle one contested point—that is—as to the parent being a Horrocks. One of that noble family may produce a rogue—this is within the range of possibility, but an *idiot* never!!! By Heavens No! That characteristic does not exist in the *genus*.

I should very much like to tell you everything curious, comical or interesting that comes within the range of my organs of observation, but a letter does not give me scope enough. I must wait till I see you before I can tell you everything. Yesterday I was occupied making reports and passes for some of the men till about five o'clock in the afternoon. At that time the men had just returned from the stables and were out on the piazza in front of the barracks amusing themselves in various ways as it was a fine evening. Presently I heard a big noise amongst them and ran out to see what was the matter. I found nearly the whole company collected (including the captain) witnessing the evolutions of two of the men who had got on a pair of boxing gloves. By and bye the orderly sergeant, a big burly Englishman who has been mate on board a ship, put the gloves on, and had a round or two with a Yankee whom he soon hammered down. Then another tried his prowess with him but with no better luck. Then the Captain, I suppose in fun, said, "Here Ross, you put them on and try him." "All right," said I, and began to spar with the lungeous giant. I soon found that he intended conquering me by sheer strength so I kept (my hat on, Dad!) cool, and when he made a tremendous lunge at my head, I ducked, and suddenly planted my right hand glove fairly in his chops. He tried to leap backwards, slipped, and fell on his—. Ah, Sir, you would 'a' lowfed. Well up he came again, but vexed this time, and his blows fell so thick and fast that it was more than I could do to ward them off, but as he was reckless, and I was *hard*, I at last succeeded in reaching a point I had several times tried at,—namely his proboscis, or snout, and that with such force that the blood trickled down his moustache. I need scarcely say that victory was awarded to me, because although I received the most blows, I claimed the first *knock down* and the first *blood*. There was one difference between his blows and mine, worth mentioning. He struck down thus . . . like a sledge hammer, and I struck straight out from my shoulder thus . . . like the delivery of a light 12 pounder shot. This was the close of pugilism for that evening.

70

After that I had supper (bread, tea and stewed apples) and then the mess room was cleared up, and all hands set to work dancing, to the music of three fiddles, a piccolo and a pair of castanets (and two kegs of Lager bier provided by the Captain). This continued till 9 o'clock with occasional songs etc. The songs were the reverse of delicate and refined, but what can you expect. I did not sing nor give any display of Ventriloquism. I reserve my *very wonderful talents* for more select society. And I assure you I will not contaminate myself by remaining in such company three years. I feel myself superior to it and consequently must soar above it, even if I risk a little in the effort.

Sometimes some of the men are punished for drunkenness etc. One mode is this. If there are two of them, one is put in a wheelbarrow and the other is made to wheel him for half an hour, and then change places. They are kept at this for about three or four hours without intermittance. Some time ago there was a drunken Irishman who got drunk beastly after often being punished for the same offense. The Captain devised a new means of punishment for him this time. He made a spread eagle of him, that is tied him with his hands and feet as far from each other as possible, and then poured buckets of water on his head. At every bucketful, the Irishman remarked in a plaintive voice, "This is nothing to what the Saviour suffered." I must say that this Christian but unhappily drunken martyr has not been found drunk since his shower bath.

In concluding, I wish I could just tell you what you most want to know about me. Perhaps you want to know how soon I am going to leave this. Well, I shall go very soon if Brady sends the box as I have instructed him to do, but if there is a likelihood of getting two months' pay, I will wait a little longer. I hope you do not blame me for skedaddling. Well, no matter, I am bound to leave, so you must excuse me in this and in everything else, always believing me to be

Your most affectionate son
James

5th New Jersey Battery Light Artillery
Gloucester Point
Opposite Yorktown
Virginia
April 22nd 1864

My Dear Parents,

You will see by this that I have not done as I intended, and I dare say you will be glad to know that I have changed my mind with regard to leaving the battery, at least in the way I then intended. I could have done so the day we left Camp Barry, and should have been successful I am sure in getting away safely, but I somehow or other began to think better of it, and the result is that I am here still and likely to remain here, for the present at least.

And now having told you the most important item, let me tell you the most interesting events that have occurred since writing my last. We, that is the Battery, on Sunday the 17th inst. received orders to march immediately. This was twelve o'clock at noon. No one was prepared for the order to come so suddenly although we had received warning the day before that we might be ordered to move in the course of a few days. Consequently everything was in confusion. Hurry-skurry, many valuable things thrown away because not absolutely necessary for a soldier. About six o'clock all was ready for the move, and then learnt that our destination was "Fortress Munroe".

We went to the government landing stage on the Potomac near Washington and there embarked in a splended steamer (horses, men and artillery). We did not leave however till morning on the 18th, about 10 o'clock. Then we set sail down the Potomac, which flows about 100 miles and then empties itself into the Chesapeake Bay. In some places it is five miles wide and in no place less than one mile except at Alexandria where there is a bridge across it 7/8 of a mile long. On entering the Chesapeake Bay we sailed south and about 11 o'clock p.m. arrived opposite Fortress Munroe, which is I suppose the largest Fortress in the U.S. We lay off here till morning, the Captain going ashore for orders, and when he came on board again it was with orders to proceed to the place you see mentioned at the heading of this letter. Yorktown is just across the river or bay from our encampment and is not only remarkable for the seige of MacClellan but is worthy of note from the fact of Lord Cornwallis having here surrendered in 1776 to Washington.* The appearance of the place as it appeared on our arrival about noon, day before yesterday, was decidedly insignificant. A few Houses are all that we can see of it, and these are mostly occupied by officers. After getting all our baggage and ordnance ashore, we remained about three hours waiting for orders as to the place to encamp. About four o'clock a stout man with black beard and moustache came up to the Captain accompanied by a Colonel of infantry.

The Captain dismounted from his horse and after being introduced to the gentleman with the Colonel, he shouted to me to come up to him. I was riding one of the lieutenants' horses at the time and when I came up the Captain told me to accompany the gentleman. The Colonel mounted the bugler's horse and the other gentleman mounted the Captain's and set off at a gallop. I followed them to an encampment about a mile from the place, and then heard the Colonel invite the gentleman to take something, and learnt from the way he addressed him that the stout gentleman with black beard etc was a General. They dismounted and entered a tent and I held their horses for about a quarter of an hour. The General then came and asked me if I had a revolver. I told him No, but I could get one if necessary. He said, Oh No, Never mind. He and the Colonel and a Captain then mounted their horses and rode along the country about another mile, where we were overtaken by an escort of Armed Cavalry. We called at every house we came to, the General making various enquiries as to the country, springs etc and about 4 miles from where we started we came up to the line of pickets (Union pickets of course). The general (General Bodges I think is his name) asked the pickets various questions and then we rode past them into what I of course considered the enemies' country. At a distance of another mile however we came up to a cavalry man, who proved to belong to another line of pickets (cavalry). We rode then right along the line of pickets questioning them as to their orders etc until we came to a creek or river which is one of the boundaries of this peninsula, for this is a little peninsula and is the beginning of the peninsula where MacClellan made his retreat. We then rode back to the tent before mentioned and I took the horses from the Colonel and General, with orders to thank our Captain for the use of them. So I rode back with the three horses, the cavalry men going in another direction. After some trouble, for it was now about 8

* A mistake for 1781.

o'clock and rather dark, I found the place where our battery was encamped.

Three of the men were called to unsaddle and see to the horses, and I turned in after supper with the orderly sergeant and the Quartermaster Sergeant who had made a very comfortable bed with the baggage under shelter of a waggon cover. We are now more comfortably fixed in a little hut built of shingles or split pieces of timber. The men live in tents made by the covers or tarpaulins of the pieces. Troops are arriving at this point very fast and most probably a grand movement is intended to be made from this point in the direction of Richmond. Oysters are very plentiful in the River and other fish can be bought very cheap here, but the sutler who is the only man we can buy anything from here, charges exorbitant prices for everything: 10 cents for a drink of cider, 25 cents for a small pie, 50 cents for an ugly little necktie etc.

I am *very comfortable indeed!*, having now nothing much to do but keep the accounts of the Company. I can take a ride out for pleasure whenever I think proper, and as I fare just as the orderly sergeant does I get the *best* of everything in the *edible* line that can be got here. For instance, the 1st Sergeant told the Cook this morning to fry some beefsteaks and onions for three and to make three good cups of coffee and after the men had finished their breakfast (coffee, bread and cold pork) the orderly and Quarter-master Sergeant and myself sat down to beefsteak and onions and coffee and bread. Tonight we are going to have some stewed oysters. I am very anxious to send you word how I am getting on in order that I may receive news from home, so in order that I may do so I will bring this letter to a conclusion in the hope that you will answer it at once. I intend to write at greater length by and by, that is in the course of a week or so. In the meantime I hope you will try to send me a letter soon, and do not have any fears for my safety. I am seeing a little of the world and adding to the stock of my information and I assure you I will take every care of myself.

In the next letter I send I will tell you everything interesting that may occur or that I may see, that is *If I can*. There is a rumour afoot here that correspondence will not be allowed after a little while, but I will write an account of anything comical or curious and will send it off to you the first opportunity. And you must send me as long a letter as you can, only do not lose any time in sending it off.

There are plenty of wild ducks in the river here. I suppose if the whole place, river, ducks and all, could be transported to England, it would be quite a rendezvous for sporting characters, fishers etc. I am in good health and spirits and remain as ever

Your most affectionate son,
James

> 5th New Jersey Battery
> 1st Division, 10th Army Corps
> Virginia
> May 8th '64

My Dear Parents,

My last was dated from Gloucester Point. Since writing it we have removed with the whole corps to this place which is in the midst of the Rebels, being about 4½ miles N.E. of Petersburg and 20 miles S.E. from Richmond.

On the 3rd inst. we embarked at Gloucester Point in steamers, taking with us our horses and pieces. We did not know which way we were about to go. Even the Captain was ignorant of the movement which was intended. We lay out on the York river till early on the morning of the 5th when the whole fleet (about 40 vessels) sailed to Fortress Munroe and thence up the James River. The country looked beautiful along the banks but although we must have sailed above a hundred miles, I was surprised not to see a solitary human being even around the houses, and we passed many. We passed Harrison's landing and City Point. About a mile above the last-mentioned place we cast anchor (about 9 o'clock p.m.).

Early next morning we disembarked. As I saw it was likely we should have to wait some time, I took a walk with another fellow. We passed several little shanties, and at every one the soldiers (Union) were ransacking and taking everything worth taking, to the great indignation of the darkies to whom they belonged. We walked on about a mile and a half and then came to a fine residence of a planter, in which about a dozen soldiers were making free with everything. Just as we (myself and the other fellow, Butterfield) came up to the gate of the house we met two other soldiers coming out, one carrying a ham and a couple of turkies over his shoulder and the other carrying a lamb with the head cut off. When we came up to the house, there was an old grey-headed gentleman sitting on the doorstep clasping his knees.

"Ah," he said, "they have taken my mules and killed my hogs and taken all my provisions. Oh, dear, dear!"

We walked in and in the first room to our right found an old lady well dressed upbraiding three soldiers who were ransacking the drawers and cupboards. A couple of nigger wenches were looking on in blank amazement. In the next room, which was extremely well furnished, was a piano. I sat down and played Home, Sweet Home! with variations.

Butterfield was looking round to see what he could find. He opened a mahogany cupboard in the corner and took a telescope out of it. I took a flute and a package of beautiful wax candles and a piece of scented soap. I found some Confederate money in notes, about $20, but the lady came in and begged me to give it to her as it would not do me any good, she said. I gave it to her of course and she thanked me for it. I was sorry for them but could not do them any good. We left then but took a shoulder of lamb along with us, which we fried the same night.

When we got back to the landing place we found our Battery just on the move and jumped on the caissons and rode along a dusty road in the rear of a few thousand infantry. We marched about 8 or 9 miles through a thickly wooded country meeting no opposition and seeing very few people, and those darkies.

The sun was very powerful and I was glad when we came to a clearing where the general commanding the division ordered us to stop. There was a log-house standing there and we had some coffee and meat cooked, watered the horses and had a rest for about two hours-and-a-half. In the afternoon we hitched the horses to the pieces and came to another clearing in the woods where we stayed for the night. We learnt that the rebels had left that place the night before and were about 3 miles ahead of us near Petersburg and that they were completely surprised by the suddenness of our arrival, as they had been expecting us to come up the York River from Gloucester Point and had made their preparations accordingly.

Yesterday there was a smart skirmish not far from us but it was only the infantry and cavalry who were engaged. We could hear the shots and shouts but could not see them for all around us is a thick forest of pine. It is said that our forces drove back the rebels and succeeded in getting to the railroad and pulled up a good length of the rails. (This is the railroad between Richmond and Petersburg.)

We came here last night and slept on the ground with our rubber blankets underneath us. This is a clearing very much like the others where we stopped, stumps of trees sticking up out of the long grass all over it. We are ready to move any moment and come into action, and I have no doubt we shall have some hot work here before long.

On the march from the river to this place I could not help feeling the advantage of artillery over infantry. A large number of the latter were plodding on before us, and every now and then we passed some poor fellow who had given out and lay on the side of the road with his knapsack and musket alongside of him and then we would pass portions of their kit, thrown away in order to lighten the load on their backs. *Scores* of blankets and overcoats, boots and shoes.

And now we are here doing nothing but taking care of the horses etc while the infantry are making entrenchments and otherwise preparing for an attack on the S. and W. sides of this clearing. They have been all day felling the timber so as to form an almost impassable barrier to the advances of an army, leaving only a road by which we can leave if necessary.

General Gillmore commands this corps and General Butler commands the Department. While at Gloucester Point, the latter held a grand review of the 10th Army Corps. He had a very brilliant looking staff of officers accompanying him. I got an excellent view of this very properly distinguised "Beast" and I assure you I think he bears out the title the Rebels or Confederates have given him both as regards appearance and character, namely "Beast Butler". I rode on the *caisson* within a yard or two of him, and as he raised his hat as I was passing (a mark of deserved deference to myself no doubt) I saw him distinctly, and can recognise him anywhere I may see him again. Call before your mental vision a sack full of muck (well filled and shaken together mind) placed on a beautiful charger (no humbug about that). And on the top of this imagine a bloated-looking bladder of lard, dressed around with oakum but polished on top; a *cock-eye* and a ferocious looking mustache in front. And then imagine four enormous German sausages fixed to the extremities of the sack in lieu of arms and legs, and you have before you a fancy portrait of Major General Butler.

I have had my hair cut close like a resident of the New Bailey in

Manchester. My face and neck have lost their chalky hue and are now approaching nearer the color of the inside of shoe leather. I am enjoying excellent health, but am not yet realising a fortune, but instead of that there is no use trying to ignore the fact that I am running a fearful risk of losing my life. But do not get out of spirits on that account. *My* loss will be the greatest, and I am sure I am not at all alarmed yet, though I have not yet felt the sensation of *uncomfortableness* which one must feel when he hears bullets and shells whistling and shrieking around him. When I have felt it, I will tell you how it is or if I am unable I will so arrange it that someone else will let you know. The mails are of necessity very irregular here and you must not be surprised if you do not hear from me in a considerable length of time. I have not heard from you for a long time. That is of course no one's fault but my own. I am very anxious to get a letter from you in order that I may know how things are progressing in your corner of the earth. And when you write you must be sure to tell me all the news. Remember that it is so long since you wrote that many things that seem old to you will be news for me.

I have not seen any newspapers lately so that I cannot tell you anything that you have not read in your own papers. That is as regards War news etc. My convenience for writing is not very good altho' I am still Company Clerk, and you must therefore excuse me if the writing is indistinct. It is the best I can do under the circumstances. You will doubtless wonder whether or not I shall have to act as a cannoneer or not. I am afraid I shall be obliged to do so.

May 17th. I am still alive and happily am still in possession of all that nature endowed me with, and this is saying a great deal when we have been under fire of the enemy for *five days* and part of the nights too. On the 11th our Battery was ordered to support an advance of this division. (As we are in the 1st Brigade of the 1st Division we are supposed to lead the van of the entire army. We advanced in a N.W. direction about two miles and there the skirmishers in advance stopped for the artillery as they had come in sight of a Company of Cavalry. Our Battery came into position and we saw the rebels about two thousand in number skirting the edge of the wood about 1,500 yards from us. We fired shell and spherical case at them and they retired. I will not say retreated because altho' I am certain some shots took effect (as we could see them burst) they took *no notice of us at all*! They did not seem to quicken their pace even.

On the 12th we advanced to the railroad and mounted one of our pieces on a car, or wagon, hitched the horses to the wagon and off we drove towards Richmond. It was my piece that was mounted and consequently I had to go along with my detachment on the car. We drove slowly you may be sure throwing out cavalry and infantry both in front and on each side to prepare us for an attack of the enemy. Very soon without any warning, *Bang, Bang, Pish, Pst*, sounded in our ears and bullets whistled past us taking effect on a few of the infantry but not touching anyone aboard the car. We opened in the direction from which came the shots, with cannister and case shot, and the rebels were very soon silenced. We however soon came to a stand-still in front of a fort, that is about a mile from it. It was armed with Whitworth English-made guns and it soon made us "advance backurts". We dismounted the piece and slept on the ground that night. The next morning we advanced right within range of the fort, formed line of battle and then commenced an artillery duel between our battery supported by the 1st Connecticut and the rebels in the fort. After 2 hours we had silenced every gun and the infantry charged the fort and took it with about 20 prisoners. I cannot tell you all that has occurred since then. We have been fighting ever since and driving the enemy back till last night which found us within 9 miles of Richmond. We have lost 14 men in killed and mortally wounded and 20 horses and last night we were ordered to come to the rear of the army in order to get a little rest for man and beast, and strange to say since we came here about 3 o'clock this morning, the rebels took advantage of the fog and rain to charge our troops. They are said to be strongly reinforced!! The result is that the rebels have again taken the ground they had lost or at least most of it.

The first time that bullets whistled past my ears I confess that my heart fluttered, but 10 minutes afterwards I did not seem to care anything about them nor for the shot and shell that buzzed past us. Part of a shell struck the wheel of my piece close to me, but a *miss* is as good as if it were a mile off.

The Confederates are a ragged kind of soldier but they fight well. There will be some desperate fighting before Richmond is taken.

(But I again beg you to suffer no apprehension for me; I think I shall come out all right.)

I enclose the daguerrotype of Capt. Z. C. Warren with his autograph on the back of it.

I should like to write you more but I am tired. I cannot buy any Postage stamps here, so I must send this without. My love to you all. God bless you. I am all right and remain

Your affectionate son
James

*May 18th.** Last night the whole camp was alarmed. I was awakened out of a most comfortable sleep by the sound of musketry. I lay still, determined not to get up unless really necessary, and as it proved to be a false alarm, I did not get up at all.

During the engagements we have had, I have witnessed several charges of the rebels and of the Union troops. It is a most exciting thing to see. At a given signal they rush forward "en masse" with fixed bayonets, and when within a certain distance of the foe, they fire and again rush forward, all the time uttering a loud continuous shout.

The cry of our troops is like a regular English shout, but the Greybacks (or Rebels) make a noise like the howl of a dog. I ought to say like a thousand dogs, or perhaps more like the war-cry of so many Indians.

On the 15th we saw some of the Rebels at about 600 yards distance along the edge of the woods. We fired into them. It seems that they had a large force in the woods at the time and our fire must have been very destructive. The shells set the woods on fire and since then 60 bodies have been found in the wood, partially consumed, which may have been done by our battery.

> 5th New Jersey Battery Lt. Arty.
> 1st Div. 10th Army Corps.
> Bermuda Hundred, Va.
> Via Fortress Munroe

My Dear Ole Dad,

I received your most welcome and interesting letter this morning, May 28th '64, and proceed right away to answer it. In the first place

* The original letter reads *Aug 18th*.

it may be interesting to know where I am. Our Battery is stationed behind a line of breastworks, extending from the James River in a Southerly direction; firing is going on all the time from the Artillery on the left of the line (We are on the right) and occasionally a shot or shell flies over us, but "*use* is second nature" and instead of being at all alarmed about it, I do not feel in the least uneasy. The rebels can be plainly discerned by anyone standing on the redoubt on the left. They are not above 400 yards from our line of pickets and yesterday some of them exchanged papers etc. These pickets do not fire at each other. It is a kind of understanding between them, because what advantage would it be to either side to murder a few pickets and lose most likely the same number themselves. It could not advance the cause or strategy of either side by doing so and consequently a kind of friendship is established, only broken when one side or the other attempts to advance. The firing I mention is only between the guns on our fort and the guns on theirs. (The lines of pickets being between the two, in rifle pits.) The Captain treats me very well. I do no duty but what little writing there is to be done for the Battery.

I kept a diary for a few days since coming behind the breastworks from which I take the following:

May 21st '64. Yesterday there was very considerable fighting going on in front of us between our line of skirmishers and those of the enemy, the latter of whom were seeking to advance, but then they wouldn't let 'em—Bow-wow-wow etc. We could see our line of skirmishers, or at least part of them, from here, but as they were in very close proximity to the enemy we could not open our guns on them for fear of injuring our own men, and consequently we were spectators and I assure you it was a very exciting sight to see them and hear the clattering banging sound of their muskets. The Confederates were drawn back finally but with considerable loss on our side. But I think the other side must have lost in that one skirmish more than we did; among others—Brig. Gen. Walker of the Rebel Army was taken prisoner, being wounded on the arm and through the leg. I was *near* the place where they brought him in and saw him and heard him speak. He asked who commanded the division and being told Gen. Terry said, "Tell him that all the prisoners who fell into my hands have been treated well," as much as to say, "And you ought to treat me well. . . ." General Walker is a fine looking man, as well as I could judge seeing him on a stretcher. His uniform was not unlike that of our British Volunteers—*Grey*, only he wore a jacket instead of a coat having three stars on the collar to indicate his rank like these * * *. An Irishman who was standing near said, "If I was one of the men carrying him I would *dump* him," meaning jolt him. Oh how I detest the breed. They are in a strong majority here or else they would get their stinking *posteriori* well kicked by the Englishmen.

At night there is quite a different scene here to any in England. The constant noise you hear all night is something astonishing. The trilling of the frogs, the whistling and chirping of the crickets, grasshoppers and whip-poor-wills makes a medley more loud than pleasant, and another peculiarity is the strange sight of little dancing lights in *millions* along the ground and in the trees, caused by flies or insects called lightening bugs. I do not know the proper name for them. (Perhaps fire-flies.) I caught one last night, and found the light proceeded from the rear part of its body. It is not constant but lasts for say 10 seconds and then disappears for two or three.

May 22nd 1864. I had just gone to sleep in my little shelter tent last night when I was awakened abruptly by rapid and vehement firing in the immediate neighbourhood. I leisurely dressed and went up to the breastworks where I found all the men standing at the guns and the infantry lining the breastworks between the guns. The fighting was about 6 or 700 yards in front of us, and to the left. We could not open fire without orders and indeed it would have been dangerous to our own men to have done so. But by and by some of the Rebel artillery opened on our left and then commenced most furious cannonading. The shells could be easily seen flying through the air like falling stars. The flashing and roaring of the guns caused a very sublime spectacle and to increase the spectacular and auricular effect the big guns on the monitors on the James River on our immediate right began to bang away in an oblique direction, throwing the shells right over the woods and into the immediate vicinity of the rebel guns. After half an hour's racket all became as still as before, and I went and fell into a sweet sleep which lasted till this morning.

May 24th 1864. Last night the Captain sent me to the landing with the mail and to bring up the mail. It is about seven miles distant by the road, and the road is despicable. Of course I was mounted and set off about 5 o'clock. I got there all right but before I started back it began to rain and rapidly to become dark. I got the mail and started. My horse was very willing and he flew over the road till it became so muddy that he could hardly trot and then he suddenly plunged into a hole that took him up to the belly in mud and water. This road was lined with a dense forest on each side and being paved with logs, had got sadly out of repair by the troops and artillery passing over it. I very soon came to a place where a small by-path turned to the right, and as it seemed to me that by taking it, I should cut off part of the road and come into it higher up where I remembered that there was a bend, accordingly I dashed into it regardless of rebels or devils and found that my nag got along *bully*, although the path was very narrow and the limbs of the trees often struck my face. But I began to notice after some time that the boughs were oftener brushing against me and the horse, and at last the horrible truth flashed across my mind that I was lost in the woods. I dismounted and felt with my hands on the ground for some semblance of a path—but No, there was no difference here between the ground where the horse was standing and that under the trees. All around was the same so I at once turned the horse's head and tried to get back to the road. I went on till I was sure that I must have travelled the distance to the road, but I had yet seen no semblance of a path, or a road, so I again dismounted, drenched to the skin, and let the horse nibble the grass and leaves for about a quarter of an hour—and then struck off again, determined to go in one direction wherever that took me to. Two hours of the most miserable riding brought me to the edge of the woods and I found to my sorrow that I was in sight of the shipping on the James River and must therefore have come back instead of going forward but even this was consolation to the misery of spending a night in the woods. I at once struck out for the road and when once on it I followed it. About 4 or 5 miles from the landing, I came to a building formerly a school-house but now occupied by an enterprising Yankee, who had come to make money by selling things to the soldiers, in other words a "sutler". There was a light here and I tied my horse to a stump in front of the building and in a shed very near I found some corn stalks, an armful of which I gave to the *fiery steed*, and then boldly knocked at the door of the school-house. It was opened by a middle-aged man with black beard and moustache, who let me in and I asked him what he had to sell. I bought some cakes and cheese from him and cider and found he had not been able to get all his things from the landing, amongst others, he had no tobacco and that he wanted a smoke badly. So I gave him some, and in return he gave me a glass of whiskey and would not take money for the other etceteras I had received; after warming and drying myself by the log-fire, I set out once more on my journey, after staying there altogether about an hour and a half. By this time the rain had ceased, and the silvery moon appeared, illuminating the scene with her soft light. I arrived in camp at one o'clock. The Captain was awake. I had brought him the *Herald & Tribune* which he commenced to read, and I retired to my fragile domicile and fell without a murmur into the welcome arms of Morpheus, and there I languidly remained till seven o'clock this morning. If I had been a cannoneer or driver or indeed anything else but a company clerk I should have been obliged to get up at half past three and stand by the gun, ready for action. If for no other advantage than this it is worth while to hold my present position. Indeed I am as comfortable and happy as a *soldier* can well expect to be. No one is my "boss" but the Captain, and he proves himself to be a very kind and good natured one.

May 29th. I have been down to the landing again today for papers and for the mail. I have also been the bearer of various despatches to several generals in difficult places. I cut quite a dash with my spurs, boots, hat and cockade, mounted on a noble charger (or as per Bro. Peter, cart hoss). The mud-crushers (or infantry) must be quite envious to see such as me and other mounted gentlemen gallop past them, while they are plodding along through the mire. Our line of pickets is within talking distance and they exchange papers, and give coffee for tobacco etc. One of our men shouted to one of theirs, "How soon do you think we shall get to Richmond, Johnny?" "Oh," said he, "you will be in Hell before you get to Richmond."

May 31st. Last night after supper I was chatting with one of the sergeants (This was about 6 o'clock p.m., the pleasantest part of the day), when I heard a yell in the distance. "There's a rebel charge, by

Jove," said I. He listened a moment and then said, "You are right. Fall in men. Prepare for action." All had been quiet for several days, and the soldiers were all taking things easy, lying in their tents smoking, reading or drinking coffee, but suddenly—*boom, bang*—went a couple of rebel guns, and two or three shells burst right over us. Then you might have seen a lively sight, hundreds of men, some only half dressed, running like mad from their tents to the breastworks, seizing their muskets and rifles and preparing for action. It seemed strange that I heard no musketry. There was artillery making noise enough but there did not seem to be any infantry engaged and I began to fear that the rebs must have suddenly charged on our line of pickets and taken them all prisoners. About two hours later all was again still, and from some of the men who came in after standing picket, I learnt that the rebels had only been just trying to find out how many guns we had. When they were about to open on us, some of the Johnnys (Confederates) shouted to our pickets and told them to lie down as they were going to open on our works with artillery. They did so of course, and consequently not one of them was injured. This may seem strange but it is nevertheless true. The fact of the matter is that although at war, there is no personal feeling of malice between the men. It is only a political difference between two sections of the country. From what you say in your letter, I should judge that the federal army were coming off only second best—and very much so too. But if you read the papers published by the Yankees, you would read there a chapter of the most brilliant successes of the Union arms. However I am so situated that I can judge for myself of what weight to attach to anything stated in our papers. When I have seen with my own eyes the Union army of General Butler driven within their own intrenchments by an inferior force of the Confederates and read next day in the paper news to the effect that Gen. Butler had played the very devil with the rebels and then as there was no convenient resting place for his forces he had *leisurely retired within his own lines*, also that the troops had the fullest confidence in General Butler and cheered him as he passed along the lines most vociferously—I can testify that only one regiment cheered him (and they must have been d—fools to do it), that there is no confidence felt in the *beast* at all, and that he would be more likely to get *hooted* than *cheered* by any regiment or Battery that I am acquainted with.

85

June 2nd. I think it is high time for me to finish this letter. In conclusion then, I am sorry that my dear mother misses me so much but I cannot now help it, at least not at present, for it is impossible to be set at liberty, only by great political influence or by sickness. Eighteen, not 21, is the age at which Americans recognise a man's free will to enter the army etc. I am glad Bro. George is all right, and with regard to the time when I am rich I assure you that I will buy you as much 'bacco as you can conveniently smoke—and mother as many new caps as she can wear.

Walter and Peter have done remarkably well in the drawing examination. I shall always be pleased to hear of their progress.

It strikes me that you and my dear mother must be two very comfortable looking, fat individuals.

June 3rd. I have nothing new to add. Only that the more comfortable and happy I know you to be, the more contented and happy I shall be. I and another fellow, the guidon or color bearer, have today built a bomb-proof habitation. If firing commences in the night we can now lay still, as we are non-combatants. I have a kind of impression somehow that I shall live through this war and come home all right.

I hope that we shall all have a Sunday dinner together yet—Bro. George and all.

With love to Sister Annie, Bro. Benjamin and to all of you—and should anyone else enquire after me remember me to them and believe me ever your affectionate son,

    A.R.

                5th New Jersey Battery
                1st Div. 10th A.C.
                In the field, Va.
                July 10th 1864

My Dear Ole Dad,

I received your kind letter referring to getting me out of the army through Gen. Grant and although I felt very certain, or I may say rather sure, of failure through such a course, I did my best to forward the movement. On June 23rd, two nights after receiving your letter, I sent off two communications, one from myself and the other from Captain Warren, to Gen. Grant—like the following:

Lt. Gen. Grant
Honored Sir,
   At the request of my parents I have the honor to make the following statement.
   I arrived in this country from England in July last, and enlisted in the above Battery on the 21st August 1863. This was without the knowledge or consent of my parents. They now write me stating that they have made application to you for my discharge and also request me to apply to you for the same purpose—on the ground of my being a minor as at present I am only nineteen years of age.
   If a discharge can be obtained I am prepared to return all govt. bounty which I have received.
   Should you condescend to notice this small affair in the midst of the greater cases resting upon you—you will have my warmest gratitude and the blessing of a good mother for whose sake alone I thus trouble you.

With great respect I have the honor to be Sir,
Your most Obedt. servant,
Andrew Ross

                              Head Qrs. 5th N.J. Batty.
                              In the field, Va.
                              June 22nd 1864

   Andrew Ross, an intelligent young Englishman, is a private in my battery and for some time has been performing the duties of Company Clerk.
   He is brave and cool in action and since he has been a member of my battery has always performed his duties faithfully and to my entire satisfaction.

Z. C. Warren
Capt. Comdg: 5th N.J. Batty.

You must know that Capt. Warren was not aware that I should send his testimonial to Gen. Grant and in fact does not know it yet. I thought better not to give him your letter for several reasons, the *principal* being that your letter to him was so worded that any shrewd man, and he is not dull, would come to the conclusion that my name was not Andrew Ross but Horrocks, and had I given the letter to him he would not only have done nothing in the matter but have felt a distrust of me, which at present he is very far from feeling; consequently instead of showing him the letter I merely told him that I should be glad if he would favor me with a short testimonial stating so-and-so. He wanted to know for what purpose and I told him that my father wanted it for something or other so he gave me the one of which you see the copy.

As I expected it all resulted in nothing not even bringing me an answer of any kind as yet.

I am in perfect good health and very comfortable. You have no idea what a snug little domicile I have got. We are still behind the line of entrenchments that I told you about, near the James River, and have only been away from them once. That was when Gen. Grant came to Petersburg. The rebels in our front left and we advanced as far as the Richmond and Petersburg Railroad which we partially destroyed but Longstreet's corps soon drove us into our holes again and here we remain, the Rebels keeping us *at Bay*.

I suppose after all they will keep Grant out of Richmond quite a while yet. They may be starved out but even that is doubtful for I hear that they are making a raid into Maryland and taking stores of all descriptions and the Shenandoah valley is open to them yet. When Richmond is taken *then* and then only will the Northerners have any reason to hope for ultimate triumph.

President Lincoln paid us a visit on the 22nd June, riding along the line of entrenchments with Gen. Butler and staff. He is a very plain man, wearing at the time a black suit. I was over in the Caisson Camp about a mile from here when he came along. I knew at once it was Old Abraham from the many likenesses I have seen of him.

As I told you in my last I have a horse for my own private use and amusement. This one is the sixth I have had, the other five being faulty in some respect or other. One was corn foundered. Another clumsy. Another was good-looking enough but not capable of bearing much fatigue.

This one of mine now is a first rater. His neck arches beautifully.

He stands straight on his pins and is 17 hands high. He can beat every quadruped that he has yet come near on the road. His mane was shaggy when we got him and was cut close, and now it stands straight up about 4 or 5 inches. The Captain wanted me to comb it on the off side but I told him No! that I liked to see him look fee-rocious. He's a heye like an ork.

Today I took a ride with one of the Sergeants as far as the River Appomattox, to the landing and pontoon bridge where Grant receives his supplies. The Christian Commission and Sanitary Commission have depots there so I went in and from the first got this paper, some religious papers and half a dozen lemons, and from the second some tobacco, some pickles and a packet of farina, all *free*, *gratis* and *for nothing*.

Talk about the horrors of war, why there is more danger, more care and more work for a citizen than there has been here for the last three weeks.

Last night I laughed till my sides fairly ached. The Captain has a coloured servant who either was or imagined himself to be sick, complaining very much of pain in his head.

The Captain turned to me while I was writing in the tent and asked me what I would recommend to Lewis. "Well, sir," I said, "bleeding is good for most anything, especially pains in the head." (I saw he was up for fun.)

"Can you perform the operation, Ross?"

"Oh yes sir. I know how to *flee* bottomize better than any of the army doctors, I assure you."

"Well then you had better do it. Get your instruments please. Come here Lewis."

"Oh no sir. You ain't a goin to bleed me. I *ain't* no horse."

"Come here you blockhead you and let Mr Ross cure you," shouted the Captain.

So the poor darky came up.

The Captain then told me I had better examine him before performing the operation, so I began plying him with questions which mystified the poor fellow completely, and set the Captain in such a state of convulsion that he rolled on his bunk as if in agony, his sides shaking and his face *shortened* but keeping the noise stifled as much as possible in order that the joke might be carried right up to the handle.

Said I, "What part of the old country are you from? How many languages do you speak fluently? Ah, you do not seem to comprehend. Where was you riz? Let me feel your pulse. Ah, a bad case etc. Stay there a moment."

I then went and got an auger to act in the place of a lance and a large ammunition box for a basin.

When the poor devil saw these preparations he suddenly expressed himself as feeling much better, in fact quite well. But the Captain, resuming his gravity as much as possible, bade Lewis to stand up and roll his shirt sleeve up. This he did and I rolled up my sleeves and prepared for action. Up to this time I had kept my countenance pretty well but the first Lieutenant quite upset me by proposing that we got a stovepipe to carry the blood into the vessel.

However I did recover myself well enough to proceed. I tied a tethering rope round his arm and made him turn his head away. Then, getting the 1st Lieutenant to hold his arm, I took the red ink bottle in my left hand and flourishing the auger in my right, I gave him a sharp prick in the arm with the end of it, and at the same time poured a little red ink on the place. "There," said I, "you are all right." He looked round and saw the *blood*. Oh! Hubbaboo. Such a row the fellow made. I laughed most heartily and after we had all regained our gravity, the Captain made it all right with Lewis with a good stiff glass of whiskey. He is all right this morning, his pain being gone quite away, he says.

Well now in conclusion let me beg of my mother not to make herself uneasy on my account. I shall not act any more as cannoneer but in the event of my being in a battle at all it will be as a mounted orderly and it will be my duty to ride along the *rear* with messages from Capt. Warren to his inferior officers and also to his superior officers. So my risk is very small.

I am living well in spite of the premium on gold. The Captain allows me to buy from the commissariat anything I want, so I get flour, molasses and many things at a cheap rate that no-one else but the officers have the privilege of obtaining. The Commissary sells:

    flour
at 4 cents a pound
      molasses
at 20 cents a quart

                    dried peaches
at 18 cents a pound
                    ham
at 18 cents a pound
                    pickles
at 20 cents a half gallon

I am living well, am well lodged, clothed and fed, and, what every beggar cannot say, am well mounted.

There is a rumour afloat but I don't scarcely believe it that we are about to leave here with the Corps for Washington.

If we do leave here now we shall do so *sometime* and you may believe me I shall yet come to see you all safe and well.

What did Sister Annie mean in her last letter by the *New Sunday School*? And what plans had you in view for me *in Wigan with my Bro. Joseph*? With best love and most hearty affection,

I am always your affectionate son
James Horrocks

                                        5th New Jersey Battery
                                        1st Division, 10th Army Corp.
                                        Bermuda Hundred
                                        Virginia
My Dear Brother Joseph,

I should have written sooner than this, but I have been very sick for the last three weeks. I have the Camp Fever and am now getting better. Every care has been taken of me and every kindness shown to me. The Captain had a number of men come down and make a bunk for me, and had them pull down the old bower in front of the tent and put a fresh one up of Cedar-Boughs. Some of the men have brought over for me Condensed Milk, Farina, Maizena and Lemons. Anything I express a wish for I get, but I am very weak and it will be some time before I am completely recovered for duty. In answer to your question as to why I enlisted, I cannot give you a satisfactory answer for I do not know why I did myself.

But now you wish to know every particular of my enlistment. I enlisted on the 21st August 1863, to serve 3 years. There is no way for procuring a discharge. The only plan I know of is to get a commission and then resign. Now there is one way you might try to get me a commission. Write a letter to the right honorable Poll Parker, Governor of the state of New Jersey, stating that Andrew Ross of the 5th New Jersey Battery had received a College Education and state as much in his favor as you can. Then if you could get any influence at all to go along with the letter I would be almost certain to get a commission. There is some *"American Houses"* in Manchester, such as Kessler & Co., Patten & Co. and some others, and an accompanying letter from one of these would make the thing pretty safe. You had better write the letter and sign it too.

We have had no fighting here since I last wrote. Everything has gone on quietly. There is one great annoyance that you can scarcely conceive. That is the immense number of flies, many of which bite. They are very troublesome indeed. There has been considerable movements been made lately by the Army of General Grant but no results appear yet. There was some fighting day before yesterday down near Bermuda Landing but the Rebels were driven back. We have been remarkably quiet. I believe we have not fired a shot nor had a shot fired at us for over a month. The Rebel raids in Maryland and disgraceful conduct of the Yankees you must have read about. They have brought as much provisions from the North as must last them some time. Then the papers state that the whole party will be captured. That was a vain hope for they all got back safe, and now they have made another raid. I don't know how they will succeed this time. A young man named Russell is doing my work as Company Clerk and is writing this letter for me. I am pretty sick of a Soldier's life and I think that the thoughts of your unhappiness at home about me increase my sickness. I should like very much to have the situation you proposed to get for me, if I can come to England, for alas there is no hopes of my being able to get to England before two years unless the war ends or I get a commission. Did you get the letter printed. I guess it was scarcely refined enough. If you did you ought to send me a copy of it. I am very glad that you are all doing so well. It took me a long time to read your letter. It was the longest letter I ever received. The changes you mention about the school are very interesting to you at home no doubt, but to me they don't form much interest. There seems to have been considerable change as regards marriages etc, especially amongst cousins. I hope the prospects are as bright as they are pictured. How is it that fat and fair (married agrees) Mary Greaves has not got married as soon as her sister? Did the wood that cousin Rachel put under her oven bring forth any little loaves yet? How about cousin Lizzie and Mrs Keeveny, and how is poor Old Man who wanted his hat made into a wide-awake.

I should like to give you a full idea of the military situation but I am incompetent to do so. The movements of Grant have been so peculiar that it was stated in yesterday's paper that the length of one line is not less than 40 miles. Grant does not appear to have done much by crossing the James river. Still he may be doing something unknown to everyone. There is one beauty in his movements. That is he keeps them secret. (In James's own handwriting:)

In writing to Gov. Parker you can sign the name Joseph Ross. It is a matter of no consequence whether Gov. Parker knows my real name or not.

This is my own handwriting but my hand trembles so I am afraid you will scarcely recognize it. Do your best in the letter line and if I get a commission it will only take a short time for me to be out of this service.

Yours very affectionately
James Horrocks

U.S. General Hospital
Hampton, Va.
U.S. of A.
Aug 31st '64

My Dear Parents,

I am getting all right very fast, too fast in fact, for if I could only remain as bad as I was when I sent Bro. Joseph that last letter, I might possibly be sent to one of the hospitals in New Jersey or New York. Once there I would wait till I was thoroughly well and strong and then you might look out for *our Jamie* once more. I like Bro. Joseph's plan first rate. I should like very much to find employment at King's Cross.

There I should be comparatively, yes entirely, safe from recognition although I am not much changed, only my skin is browner. I think I told Joseph in that last letter that Cap. Warren was unwilling to send me to hospital but a movement was made across the James River, and most of the infantry was withdrawn from around us. Our doctor was sent with them, and at the end of a week after (during which time I was without a doctor), I did a bit of scheming. I called the Captain and told him that I felt a great deal worse, that I had a pain in my side and I thought I had the piles (a common complaint among the men of our battery. At least about a dozen have had them.)

I am sorry to say that what I told him was not true. However it had the effect I wanted it to have. He sent for an ambulance or four-wheeled-two-horse-spring-carriage and sent me and a man three times worse than myself to the 10th A.C. Hospital. There the patients are in tents and are not very well attended.

I knew that a Dr Buckley who had formerly attended our battery, was somewhere in the hospital and when I heard that a number of patients were being sent to Fortress Munroe, I wrote him a note asking him to send me as I thought the change of air would do me good. The nurse took the letter to him, and *five minutes* after, the doctor came to me and told me I should go that morning. I went on the steamboat on the Appamattox that morning and they brought us all the way down the James River to Fortress Munroe but there the hospitals are full so they brought us here. I take no medicine but a glass of ale every day, but they feed me so well here that I cannot help getting better, *that is stronger*. When not sick I am only weak. This morning besides bread, ham and coffee, they brought me an egg. At dinner time besides bread, beef soup and beef steak (the regular ration) I had some custard.

I shall try to get sent North and if I cannot I shall try and stay here as long as possible. Perhaps I can stay till the battery gets into winter quarters and perhaps by that time peace may be made. When you write direct it to the battery as usual, as, if I am not there they will forward my letter to where I am.

4th Sept. I am still on the fattening system, still improving. They have stopped bringing me eggs I am very sorry to say.

Tell Brother Joseph (but you don't need as I guess he will read this himself) that I enlisted for three years, and this day I have served one year and 14 days. Getting a substitute for two years would cost considerable. $600 are offered to men for one year's service, so that getting a substitute is out of my power.

A discharge cannot be bought from Govt. It might be obtained through political influence, and I have none. Consequently my plan for the future is simply this. Wait till I can get North, and if I don't get sent from here, I may get a furlough from the Battery, and then if I have money come on the first steamer. If not I will come as an ordinary seaman.

I am anxious to get out of the service myself. There are two men in beds not far from me with parts of their genitals shot off, and I cannot help thinking that I would much rather be shot through the head. (Both are disagreeable things.) Excuse any more just now, I feel rather tired.

5th Sept. I am afraid my chance of being sent North is not very good but as soon as I am strong enough to go back to the battery I am pretty sure I can get one of the doctors here to employ me as clerk for a few weeks at least and that will bring us up to the Presidential election. MacClellan seems to be the popular candidate, and peace may be made. If not, I may get a furlough from the hospital. But after all these are mere possibilities. What you may expect as the worst is that I shall be sent back to the battery. Well what if I am. I have been above a year in it and I am all right yet. This campaign is nearly over with, may be quite over before I join the battery.

I cannot answer all the letters I got in the last. I am glad my dad is doing a bit of something and that Bros. Joseph, William and Henry are all doing well. I think Mr Knox justified in bettering himself if he can. And I justify myself if I can do the same either by hook or crook.

One reason I do not want you to let it be known that I enlisted is that I would not have it known that I deserted. Tell Miss Mort I cannot get my photograph here.

With love to all, and hoping my mother may not fret herself any more for the present about me, I remain as ever

Your own
Jamie

U.S. Gen. Hospital
Hampton, Va.
Septr 17th 1864

My Dear Parents and Sister and Brothers,

I have lost hopes of my being sent North. I did think at one time that I could scheme it, but alas! circumstances proved adverse (that is I got well too fast) so that the bright visions and hopes that swelled in my buzzum were blasted. (Blast it.)

I received my dad's letter dated Aug 1st about 10 days ago. The Captain sent it to me. He also sent me two dollars, being a part of a debt to myself. The officers of this army are supposed to find their own grub, that is to pay for it and "Commisaries" are appointed by Govt. to sell them the necessaries of life at very little over cost price.

Luxuries—e.g. butter, eggs, fruit, etc—they buy from the sutler. Well our officers, except the Captain, have been promoted from the ranks, and as the pay is very tardy in coming, they are as poor as church mice. So the Captain was almost obliged to run the mess, that is, to pay for the grub, and one day when he and I were alone in his tent, he said, "I think you have plenty of money have you not?" "Well, Captain," said I, "I have about twenty five dollars." So he asked me to loan him some till payday. I lent him twenty dollars, keeping nine for my own individual expenses. The Captain then told me that he had spent so much money on the mess that he could not run it any longer and that each of the four lieutenants must look out for himself. And so they had to, and each one was obliged to sponge on the Company. Well it is a d—d shame that they are not paid punctually.

The Captain owes me 17 dollars now and I know he cannot pay it till he himself is paid and the U.S. Govt. owes me $90.00 net cash for six months' pay not to mention the 17 days that have gone in this month.

And yet, with all this paper owing to me which is worth about $50 in gold at yesterday's price, I have only 15 cents in my pocket.

Since writing my last letter I have been transferred to the Wooden wards. All the buildings or nearly so are of wood. There is very little difference between the treatment here and that in the tents. I am getting to have a ravenous appetite, and yesterday after dinner (one slice of bread and fish and one potatoe) I went to a "shanty" a few hundred yards from here, kept by a big fat negress, and ate two

A Union Army Recruiting Poster; about 110,000 volunteers from
New York enlisted during the course of the war

VOLUNTEER ENLISTMENT.

STATE OF *New Jersey*

TOWN OF *Jersey City*

I, *Andrew Ross* born in *Bolton* in the State of *England* aged *21* years, and by occupation a *Bookkeeper* Do HEREBY ACKNOWLEDGE to have volunteered this *Twenty first* day of *August* 18*63* to serve as a **Soldier** in the Army of the United States of America, for the period of *THREE YEARS*, unless sooner discharged by proper authority: Do also agree to accept such bounty, pay, rations, and clothing, as are, or may be, established by law for volunteers. And I, *Andrew Ross* do solemnly swear, that I will bear true faith and allegiance to the **United States of America,** and that I will serve them honestly and faithfully against all their enemies or opposers whomsoever; and that I will observe and obey the orders of the President of the United States, and the orders of the officers appointed over me, according to the Rules and Articles of War.

Sworn and subscribed to, at *Jersey City* this day of *August* 18 *63*

Andrew Ross

BEFORE

I CERTIFY, ON HONOR, That I have carefully examined the above named Volunteer, agreeably to the General Regulations of the Army, and that in my opinion he is free from all bodily defects and mental infirmity, which would, in any way, disqualify him from performing the duties of a soldier.

D. L. Reeve M.D. EXAMINING SURGEON.

I CERTIFY, ON HONOR, That I have minutely inspected the Volunteer, previously to his enlistment, and that he was entirely sober when enlisted; that, to the best of my judgment and belief, he is of lawful age; and that, in accepting him as duly qualified to perform the duties of an able-bodied soldier, I have strictly observed the Regulations which govern the recruiting service. This soldier has *Blue* eyes, *Brown* hair, *Light* complexion, is *5* feet *7* inches high.

5th Battery New Jersey Artillery Regiment of Volunteers,

Z. C. Warren RECRUITING OFFICER.

GOV. PRINT. OFF. July, 1862.

James Horrocks's Volunteer Enlistment. He gives his name as Andrew Ross and his age as 21 (he was 19).

Above: A letter sent to James from Joseph, redirected from Richmond to Texas.

Right: Jamie's *Carte de Visite* in his uniform of the Fifth Battery New Jersey Volunteers.

Broadway and Spring Street, New York City, as Jamie would have known them.

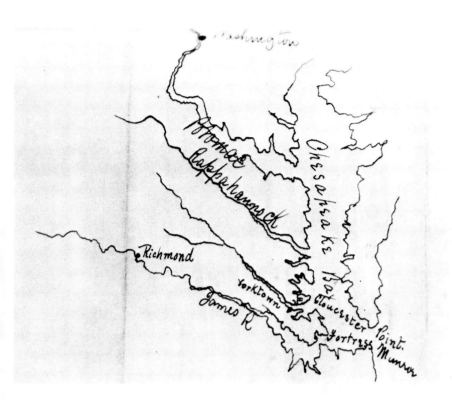

Above: Jamie's map of the peninsula of Virginia, where he spent much of the war.

Right: One of Jamie's early letters home.

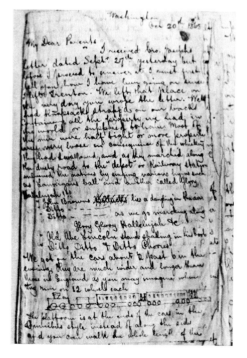

The ruins of Richmond after the Union Army victory in 1865.

Jamie's brothers and sister: *left to right* Peter, Annie, Joseph, Ben and Walter, circa 1897.

Jamie on a visit to England in about 1895, with brothers Peter and Walter.

"Appo-pastits" and drank two strong cups of coffee for which I only paid 20 cents, which is remarkably cheap, but alas! I have now only 15 cents, and *that* I must keep for an emergency. I would write to the Captain to send me another dollar but the return post, so badly are things managed and so many letters are sent to and from the army, would take seven or eight days, and by that time I shall be either sent back to the battery or detailed for some duty in the hospital, at least I think so. If I had money I should buy something to eat every day. Eggs and custard and milk porridge have now been strangers for more than a week. . . . The word *Salmon* in dad's short letter made my mouth water. As for filling Coal pits in Wigan, that's a job for leatheryeads, and as for theigho t'durt dehn at bothom, why mon, what's use a gerrin a little chap like me when they can get Mestre *Ox*,—weighin 11 score 13½ lbs and a few oz for two children for two shillin a wick less.

I see very few white folks outside the hospital but there seems to be some hundreds of niggers living in little wooden shanties. They are a merry lot, always cheery.

I am afraid I shall have to send my letter without stamp this time as I have no more on hand. Here I could not buy them if I had the money. I very much dislike to send it without. In the first place, 24 cents or say a quarter is not more to me than 2½d is to you or if I was in N. York than 5d or 6d. For instance, I must pay 5 cents for a box of matches, 10 cents for three of these sheets of paper, about a ha'porth of candy for 5 cents, Newspaper 5 cents etc. The coffee etc. that I got from the fat negress with gold (?) earrings was the cheapest thing I have bought for a long time. And in the second place I am very much afraid that I cannot put a shilling's worth in one letter, so that sending you a letter without stamp goes against the grain, or to use a Yankee expression it chafes like the very devil.

The letter I sent to my Bro. Joseph must have made my dear mother and indeed all of you sorry on my behalf. I almost repent having sent it. But after all you will feel more satisfied if you know I always tell you the worst as well as the best, which I promise you to do.

Sept 19th. I was thinking last night how it would be if I came home (and I can assure you I have a remarkable vivid imagination). The following was my first go:

I get my pay, get home, say about Christmas, have a jolly time with you all, and then through the influence of my Bro. Joseph get a sitioation in Wiggin. My mother, bless her, is very open-hearted, and by and by, she confides the little secret to some very trustworthy friend over a cup of tea, the fact that eawr James is in England again. Poor owd Mrs Hamer, a widow with a lot o' helpless chilther and not even a spare bed, but has "*a big* sthrung un" that howds *two* sometimes but *shoo's monny freinds*, and at last of all through that universal but invisible medium gossip or through the "thousand and one" accidents of life, this dear old *wretch* and of course everybody else would know it and the result is that I should

> "either be cadged for brass that I won't pay,
> or take the alarm and flee away (Shaksp—)
> It strikes me very forciblay,
> 'twd be as weel to stop in Americay." (Church Catm.)

If I was in London the case would be better one way and worse in another. I should be *free* in that world of a city, running no danger at all so to speak of an apprehension or arrest. But again, what I and you should, I am sure, feel rather bad, would be the small no. of times we could see each other in a year. But certainly it would be twice and maybe more. And even the danger of apprehension or rather I ought to say an apprehension, not for any murder or robbery but for a paltry sum of money, the net sum of which is at present £9 8s. 4d. I have the legal order before me. If she has taken out warrants regular, the expense of these would make it something more. That is the worst.

Well if I did not like to pay it I should go to prison for a month, but if I was in a good position, and could sacrifice so much money, well! paying the debt would set me entirely at liberty for that *once*. But I have dwelt on that disagreeable subject too long already. What am I talking about. Here I am in the d—d American army and am talking forsooth of being arrested by one of Mrs Hamer's monny friends while *threighdin* that dirt at bottom o' that coal pit (Mr Ox being found too heavy for any rope in Wigan).

Fortress Munroe

P.S. While in a drug store yesterday the druggist told me that a Mr O'Dell said he knew me; I replied that if Mr O'Dell ever knew me anywhere I should be much pleased to meet him. While talking, Mr

O'Dell entered and was introduced to me. He said I have never met you before but I think I knew a man who must have been related to you as he spelled his name the same way and was an Englishman. His name was Henry Horrocks and he lived at Augusta, Hancock Co., Illinois.

I told Mr O'Dell that said Henry Horrocks was my uncle and in answer to my enquiries he told me that he (Mr O'D.) was a native of Illinois, and his mother lived there at Augusta now. He, Mr O'Dell, left there in 1856 but has heard from home regularly since that time. He said that Mr Horrocks was a partner in a store when he left—He never met my grandmother but knew she was there.

Nothing more of interest.

J.H.

(You see how I keep spinning this longer.)

(When I began my letter I had not sold my shirt.)

Well I bought about 50 cents worth of sweet cakes, ginger bread. About 20 small ones which I ate that night and drank up my coffee. The next morning we were taken to another place without breakfast, and after waiting for the official as usual, who probably was "gone tut little heawse" we were taken to the Railway station, and as it was then 9 o'clock a.m. and we would have to wait here till near ½ past 11, I thought I would try and at least minister to my craving appetite even if I could not stop my bones from aching, which you may believe me was the case with sleeping first on the deck of the transport and second on the ground, this after a soft bed of hay in hospital.

The guard allowed me to go, and after going some distance without being able to get any tea or coffee I came to a baker's where I got some buns and warm rolls of bread. Well I should have starved till night if I had not got the $2.00 for the shirt. Well! I got on the railway car and rode to a place somewhere in rear of the Army, but the line is yet incomplete and instead of being able to land soldiers in rear of part of the line, I and the rest were all obliged to walk a distance of about 6 miles. At least I know I had. A guard showed the way for me and a few more to the 1st Div. of the 10th Corps and then I was shown the direction of the battery and found my way alone.

Arrived at 5½ p.m. Captain glad to see me. Is very ill himself. Asked me ordinary questions. Got good supper from his darkie, and then turned in with Russell and Vallade for the night. Received

Bro. Joseph's letter before retiring to rest. Couldn't read it for want of a light till dawn next morning and then devoured the *hulk* and thought, well I must finish my letter now and send it off. So here goes for a finish. I thank Bro. Joseph for his very clear and interesting account of his and Bro. Henry's tour. To take the trouble to write 24 close written pages for the amusement and edification of his brother is a *task of love* that I appreciate. Of course I take my old position as Clerk and Russell who is doing the work goes as corporal.

I think Coz. Mary Greaves and family are prospering to afford trips to Scotland. With love to all, I am still your own

James

> 5th New Jersey Battery
> Artillery Brigade 10th A.C.
> November 6th 1864

My Dear Bro. Joseph,

I received a letter from our glorious old dad yesterday as well as three papers containing a very interesting and pleasing account of the opening of the Farnworth Park, and I suppose I ought to answer that as well as the one you sent me a while ago, but as it is all in the family, I suppose I may kill you both with one stone—No—I mean I will kill two birds with one letter—No—that is not right because you are not birds, and I don't want to kill you. Well to proceed.

I think when I last wrote to you the Battery was in front of Petersburg. Since then we have changed camp about 12 times, and are now encamped about 7 miles South East of Richmond. The guns are in a fort some distance in front of where I am. I stay down here, in the rear, with the Caissons or ammunition carriages and the horses and drivers. On the 7th Ult. we were farther in front than where we are now and on that morning a charge was made by the Rebels which had well nigh proved successful. Everything was quiet and the first warning I had of danger was a few reports of musket firing by the pickets. I was asleep at the time, it was before dawn, and before I had time to open my eyes and get properly awake the occasional shots had increased to a perfect and continual roar.

Then "Boots and Saddles" was sounded by our bugler. I hurried to saddle my horse and the men to harness their horses and while doing so a shell burst right over my head and pieces of it struck the ground at a little distance from me. Very soon the Commanding officer found that the rebels had obtained range of us, for the shells and shot came thick and fast, so the order was given to move with the caissons to the rear and we *moved*. By Jove! We *skedaddled*.

Of course as I told you before I am a *non-combatant*, and mounted on a first-rate mare I just felt as brave as a young bull or rather a young "Ox".

The way we moved was along a path blocked by stumps of trees, and tremendous holes or ruts by no means facilitated our movements. Shot and shell were flying around us sometimes striking a tree and felling it very neatly, and sometimes striking the ground quite close, but up to this time no loss at all—only one man wounded. But all at once, when in a narrow part of the path, one of the wheel horses in one of the leading caissons was smashed by a solid shot, bringing the whole line to a stand still, and before the harness could be cleared and a spare horse put in his place another horse was shot. This took some time also to get the carriages in motion again and then we started at a trot but had not proceeded far when one of the wheels struck against a tree and smashed.

A spare wheel was soon replaced, and off we went again but before we got out of range of the enemy's guns we had lost six horses and broken three caissons. This I am afraid is only a tame description of that skedaddle but if you could only imagine the excitement and confusion which prevailed and the cursing and swearing of the men, and the "din of war" which was decidedly close. Well I say if you could imagine it, you would have a lively picture before you if not a pleasant one. However we at length got to an open clearing behind a clump of pine trees where the caissons stopped, waiting for orders. You must know that our pieces had been blazing away at the rebels all this time and in fact had driven them back, and as soon as we had arrived at this place a messenger came to say that more ammunition was wanted so we sent a few caissons to supply them.

I must now diverge a little and tell you that Capt. Warren was away from the Battery at this time and not only away but in arrest under charge of using and changing Government horses and also of breaking his *parole de honor*. He was in the Hospital of the 10th A.C. at this time suffering from "fever and ague". I had seen him a few days before this and told him that a Lt. Metcalf of the 3rd Regt.

of Rhode Island Artillery was in command of the battery and also told him that the various records of the Battery had been inspected by him and also that inspections had been made of the government property for which he (Capt. Warren) was responsible etc, etc. I told him everything I knew—as to what evidence I thought would be brought against him, and also advised him if he thought he could not refute the evidence, to resign his commission and raise another Battery and make me a lieutenant. He said he thought he could disprove the whole of the charges to be brought against him and, before I left the hospital to return to the battery, he told me to take care of his mare and horse equipment and gave me $5.00 of what he owed me. So that I was at the time I have previously mentioned mounted on a very handsome and spirited mare with a silver mounted saddle and bridle. I had also a cap of the captain's on my head and had on a very neat suit of uniform, so that if anyone did not happen to look at my shoulders to see what rank I held, he would most certainly take me for an officer.

I make this explanation in order that you may understand how it was that I was allowed to go from place to place at my own option. After the caissons had reached the place I have mentioned I took the liberty of leaving them in order to see and learn more of what was going on.

We were then a little to the North of Dutch Gap and not very far from the James River. I rode in a direction which I should judge to be about East by North, keeping far enough to the rear of the breastwork to be clear of the bullets but also near enough to see and hear what was going on.

Well I can just tell you it is very interesting to see the rear of a fighting army, perhaps more interesting and certainly more safe than to witness the operations right in front.

One thing that struck me was a complete line of men from one side to the other with loaded muskets, and with orders to shoot any man who attempted to get to the rear without pass unless he was wounded or unless he was carrying a wounded man.

At one place I came to a place where there were a number of ambulances and surgeons, and wounded men constantly arriving; in many cases an amputation was necessary to take place at once. One poor fellow with his thigh shattered by a shell I saw go through the operation.

All the wounded men were apparently attended to as well as circumstances would permit and then sent down to the landing in ambulances and placed on board the transports on the James River to be carried down to the hospitals at Fortress Munroe.

At another place I came to a place where a "Commissary of subsistence" was preparing to send provisions to the Regiments in front. Two or three cows had just been slaughtered and were cut up. I asked the Commissary for a cow's heart which he gave me and I then returned to camp.

But I cannot tell you all I saw. I met many men coming from the front, some wounded and some who had schemed it well enough to get to the rear. I asked these in most cases how things were going in front and it is surprising what different impressions seemed to prevail. One cavalry man who seemed scarcely able to keep his seat on the horse said, "We are giving them Hell!!" An infantry man who did not seem to be wounded at all (the cavalry man had blood running down his face and neck) said, "By Jesus Christ the rebels are whipping us this time."

The fact is a man who is fighting can tell you very little about the fight only as far as he is himself concerned and it is as interesting and almost as new to him to read the newspaper accounts as it is to a silly villian (civilian).

Where the Battery is staying now we have been about 10 days, and I suppose it is probable that we shall stay here for the winter. Already we are beginning to put up winter quarters; which consist of log huts.

You would be surprised to see how soon a metamorphosis is accomplished. Where trees are standing thick with undergrowth today, you may see a neat row of log huts tomorrow. Inside we have dug down about a foot so that we can stand up in any part of the shanty. The fire is on the ground just in the corner and a chimney made of two empty barrels serves the purpose very well.

For a bed we have two supports driven into the side of the shanty and long, thin sticks are laid across these, side by side, quite close. Over these we lay empty corn sacks and hay if we can manage to steal it. Then put a rubber blanket over that and a woollen blanket and an overcoat completes this very comfortable bed. Talk about your feather beds or your flocks—Je-rusalem I sleep as comfortably on this kind of an arrangement as you ever did on the softest of beds.

But sometimes we get an awful fright. The stillness of the night and our sweet slumbers have more than once or a dozen times been disturbed by the hated sound of the bugle shrill and piercing.

At the sound of the Bugle Call—"Boots and Saddles"—every man is supposed to jump up out of bed, fold his blankets (his knapsack is supposed to be packed), harness his horses and prepare everything for an immediate move. Sometimes we have had to move on at very short notice in the night time, but more often the alarm proves false. That is the expected attack does not take place, and so after standing in readiness to move (all but striking the tents) till morning light appears, we are ordered to unharness again.

Now of late I seem to have had an intuitive perception of what the thing is going to be, a move or a false alarm, and if I have the impression that no move will take place I lie still and neither saddle my horse nor fold my blankets but just take things cool, and the beauty of it is that being in the position I am no one says a damn word to me nor interferes with me in any way but the Commanding Officer himself who, I ought to tell you, is a young, well educated *gentleman*, from Providence, Rhode Island. I spend the greater part of the day in his company and his conversation is both lively and entertaining.

He has travelled through most every part of the States, North and South, and can not only describe things as he has seen them, but also relates plenty of amusing anecdotes. He has a darky for a servant that he brought with him from South Carolina. His name is William and he is what I call a good-looking nigger. He was a house servant down south and of course considers himself one of the nigger aristocracy.

Last night he had been to see one of his coloured friends in a neighbouring regiment and arrived here, apparently as usual, but in reality was slightly "tossicated." Lt. Metcalf saw at once that such was the case and he called him to him. "William," said he.

"Yes sir," said William.

"Stand up straight."

"Yes sir."

"Spell—bat."

"B. A. T.—bat, sir."

"Right William. I thought you wanted your head screwing on

tighter but I find it will do at present. Now sir, tell me the truth. Are you drunk?"

"No sir," said William.

"Have you had anything to drink?"

"Yes sir. George gub me a drink of whiskey. I tells you the trufe, sir, coss I know you'd liefer have me tell you de trufe as a lie."

"All right then. Go to bed," said Lt. Metcalf, "and sleep it off or else a darkie of about the same complexion as yourself will be missing tomorrow morning."

The battery was paid off about a fortnight ago and besides my pay—which would have been $90 but a few dollars were stopped on account of my having drawn over my allowance—I received the remaining $10.00 which the Captain owed me, and a few other outstanding debts which put over $100.00 in my pocket. Out of this I paid the sutler what I owed him and also bought several articles of necessity, including a box of paper collars and a box of blacking. I like to be decent when I am with the commanding officer most of the time.

As to the news that my father reports—of the South whipping the North from one end of the army to the other, especially the 10th Army Corps, and that Gen. Butler is killed—why it's a *damn lie*.

The Southern Confederacy is a gone goose. It is a fabric rapidly caving in and, like the fabric of a vision, it will vanish and leave no wreck behind. Yes sir, you may depend upon it that the federals will eventually be successful. The resources of the North are too much superior those of the South to admit the reasonable expect of an independent Confederacy.

There is too much at stake for the North to leave off fighting—and I think myself they are bound to win. I may be mistaken but such is my humble opinion.

Nov 10th. Last night we had another false alarm. I lay still and took it cool but I suppose every other member of the Battery lost about three hours sleep. I believe the reason of the disturbance was that the Rebels were massing their forces on the left and an attack was expected by our side. I hear that "Honest old Abe" is re-elected. Of course all the returns have not been made from the various states.

105

But so far as they have been reported Lincoln seems to be booked for another four years. All right, I do not suppose it would make the slightest difference to me whether it be Geo. B McClellan or Abraham Lincoln, so I feel indifferent about it. In the language of Old Daniel Webster, "Let em Rip".

Tell my dad there is no cotton in these diggins. If peace were made, I might possibly get into that line but I would go down South for the purpose. Virginia is not a cotton growing state—Tobacco is a staple production in this state—but of course there is no trace of it where an army is or where it has been. Like a plague of Locusts—desolation marks the track of an army.

Desolation and ruin: Nice brick houses, the residences of comfortable families probably, a short time ago, are now razed to the ground and the bricks used to make chimneys for log shanties. Corn fields trodden down and laid waste—the only trace left to show that they were ever corn fields but the regular furrows.

I am glad that the *devils* are doing so well—and not less so that Bro. William has had such an amazing success.

If I was home now I should just *enjoy*, but stop that is only a very weak word to use. I should revel in the pleasure of some flear cakes warm just baked by my blessed mother, and some nice coffee with milk in it and sugar to suit my sweet tooth and being as how I'd come home some nice tender beefsteak and "Some moor gravy."

Eh mon, awm a whoam. That's just how I'd feel. Well, never mind. It'll all come right yet. Let us all live happy. I believe in enjoying life. Yes I do, By Jove, tho' I have seemed to take a queer way of doing it, a most tarnation queer way—but 'pon my word I have had more pleasure and less of misery than generally falls to the lot of us poor mortals. Look at any of the families that we knew and tell me if you think there is one to come up with ours on point of happiness and concord. Is there such a fund of humour and love of fun, or can any such roar of laughter be raised in any other family than the one that has often been all together in Davenport Cottage. No, By Jingo! I don't believe there is. If there is, so much the better. Let em Rip. And in the language of the learned Shakespeare, D.D., "Cheer up Sam nor *let your spirits* go down."

Well here I am yet, down to the 24th page. I think I had better close this epistle. I enclose the Phot' of Pres' Lincoln for that pretty sister of mine. Ugly as sin.

But as I said before I must close but be assured, I remain always your boring brother

James

> 5th New Jersey Battery Lt. Arty.
> Artillery Brigade, 10th A.C.
> United States of America
> Nov 19th 1864

My Dear Parents,

Agreeable to your request I again, to use the stereotyped phrase, take up my pen to write these few lines hoping you are in good health as this leaves me at present, all except "Towzer" and he has got the "Bow-wow-wow el Complaint".

I am expecting in a week or two (see Annie's letter) to get a Lieutenancy in a Coloured Regt. of Infantry. What do you think about it? Chances of being shot greater; Accommodations and comforts generally smaller, but pay much larger than what I have now. No horse to ride but a uniform to wear. And above all—an *Officer's* real shoulder straps and the right of being addressed and treated as a gentleman, with the advantage of better society, and if I like it, this is a position I can hold for life, being United States troops while Volunteers will undoubtedly be disbanded when the war is over—but I would like to know if it is likely to be over soon. So would you, and undoubtedly *thousands* would give *thousands* to be able to give the date of its termination.

Uncle Abraham is again elected by Uncle Sam, and there is every prospect of a long and bitter struggle. The Federals are bound to go in and win, and the Confederates have everything to lose and nothing to gain by giving in. So that a great deal of fighting is to be expected. I will send you newspapers rather oftener than I have hitherto done, and I should like you to send me papers pretty often. *The London Times* and a few other leading papers would be very acceptable.

We have got into our winter quarters, a neat row of log huts with brick chimneys having been erected. The brick came from a kiln near the Darbytown road left by the rebels but although they have been a good deal of trouble to erect I am afraid we shall not stop in them. Of course it will not matter to me if I get the commission I expect but if not I shall be sorry to leave them. It is said that the 10th Army Corps is to have a Winter Camp in North Carolina and South Carolina. If that be so I shall probably see more of the country than I have yet.

Lt. Metcalf, the commander of the Battery vice Captain Warren, is a very pleasant fellow. He thinks well of me and tells me all about his family affairs and boyish adventures, reads me some of his letters from young ladies in the North etc, etc and in return I give him some pretty good stories of my youthful life, none of which made him laugh so much as the one (which I told him confidentially) which led to my being in his large country. He said it was considerably more interesting than any play he had yet had the pleasure of witnessing.

I also made him laugh most heartily by the relation of a certain adventure that my Bro. Henry and I and John Wright were the principal characters involved. If Bro. Harry has forgot one item of that glorious incident Bro. Jamie remembers it all.

As I told you before, Capt. Warren received the sentence of a General Court Martial on the 12th inst. which read as follows, "To be cashiered and to forfeit all pay and allowances that are or may become due to him." Special Order No. 141 Std.Ins. of General Butler.

He is now in Washington endeavouring to get re-instated but I am afraid he will fail. For my own part I should much prefer Lt. Metcalf for a Captain and I believe he has influence enough to get it.

Nov 20th 1864. Today is rainy. It has been raining since yesterday morning almost without cessation, and already the winter of Virginia begins to commence. This season is characterized chiefly by perpetual rain, and penetrating cold that pierces through one's clothing and makes one shiver. Mud of a sticky character takes one up to the knees and it is no rare occurrence to get up to the middle in it. Of course it is very easy (Oh yes) to have your boots in a fine polish all the time.

Thank goodness I have a nice warm log shanty to live in. A Battery (the 4th N.J.) that left here about a fortnight ago for New York in order to prevent anything like a riot during the election time there, returned last night and I really pitied the poor devils. Mud from top to toe, rain coming down as if Jove had turned the spiggot of his rain-barrel and gone to sleep leaving it running. Not a dry place or even a clean place to sleep. All they could do was spread the sheets or tarpaulins over stakes and poles and crawl under them.

While in New York forty of their men deserted (about one third of the whole company) and I dare say the remainder wished last night that they had followed suit. The fighting season is now nearly over for the year. The state of the ground renders the movements of Artillery almost impossible. A winter campaign may be made in N. and S. Carolina and it is said that the 10th A.C. will be the one to make it. But I think we are now tolerably safe not to go, but of course cannot feel quite sure on such a point as an important movement like that is always made suddenly and the more it takes the rebels by surprise the better.

Next Thursday the 24th inst. is to be a great day in the U.S. being the last Thursday in November. It is the National Thanksgiving Day, instituted by the pilgrims who first colonized New England to render thanks to Providence for the safe gathering in of abundant crops. They say it is an ill wind that blows good to nobody and it is also very true that it is a good wind that blows no harm to anybody.

The poor turkeys suffer in this case. Everybody must have roast turkey for dinner on that day, so a general massacre of those innocent birds generally takes place.

This year no less than forty thousand are to be killed, dressed, roasted and shipped from New York for the benefit of the soldiers, who will demolish them quick enough no doubt. I hope to come in for my share.

Nov 21st. It is still raining and does not seem to grow tired either. You mention Bro. George as likely to be at home at Christmas. I should dearly like to be at home with you, but as that is most improbable I hope you will enjoy a Good Christmas for my sake and if you have any hot Punch, Drink to the health and success of the absent but not forgetful one.

The "*Devils*" I hope are still steadily performing their good work. I think if they work you into a state of "Independency" they ought to be christened over again and instead of calling them fallen angels we might very appropriately term them "angels of mercy".

You have never mentioned a certain uncle of mine nor his family in any of your letters. The following phrase will bring him vividly to your memory: "Happy day!!! Happy Land. This is a *glorious* country." And if you do not know who I mean just look at this . . . and you will see him as he used to be when about to communicate some startling fact relative to Lord Palmerston or Johnny Russell.

I will now conclude with best love to all of you, and to Miss Betsy Mort of course.

And here goes for a finish. Yours truly, duly and tooraluly always and for ever affectionately,

Bartholomew Alexandrew
James R Horrocks

5th New Jersey Battery
Arty. Brig. 25th Army Corps
Army of the James, Va.

My Dear Parents,

Today I am twenty-one as today is the 15th of December 1864, and I have been informed by those who ought to know that I came into this sublunary world on the 15th December 1843, which was I believe wet and dreary enough. On this point however I may say that although I myself was present at the time, it is so long ago that I can not say with certainty what kind of weather prevailed. But one thing is certain, regardless of wind or sunshine I made my debut into general society, and probably made as much noise in the world as my youthful organs of respiration would permit, and what more could anyone expect. Now, in the course of human events I have attained my majority as most people do who live long enough, unless they have very bad luck. Yes, it is so. I, this day, am entitled to all the hereditary titles and entailed property which in our family descends from father to son, from generation to generation. Need I say that the gigantic proportions of my inheritance is almost over-whelming and I am compelled to give vent to my feelings in words. The people here are so profoundly ignorant that they do not know the importance of this anniversary and instead of ringing church bells and enjoying an extra good dinner, and getting slightly ele-vated (à la Ben Brust) in honor of this my natal day, they do not seem to take the slightest notice or exhibit the most casual interest in it whatsoever. This treatment I denounce as contemptuous and disrespectful, and in revenge I propose, as the toast of the evening, "Health and happiness to myself, success to my friends, and confusion to my enemies, and may the Lord have mercy on their sinful souls. Amen."

I am in good health and spirits and sincerely hope you are all well at home. I am afraid that you cannot be all right or else you would certainly have written to me before this. This is the third letter I am writing to you since receiving your last, so it is about 6 or 7 weeks since I heard from you. What can you say for yourselves. I am getting quite mad about it and I am not going to *jow my yed* but I intend to *pur* every one of you, if ever I set my eyes on you again.

In my last letter I mentioned a prospect I had of getting a commission in coloured troops. I have not seen Col. Armstrong who promised it to me since Thanksgiving Day the 24th Nov. and he told me then that he had no doubt as to the *success* of his application for me but how long it would take he did not know. It might be three or four weeks—longer or shorter.

Decr 16th. I took a ride today as far as Dutch Gap where a canal is in course of preparation, which is expected to be a great auxiliary in the reduction of the city of Richmond. When I was down there before, about three weeks since, there was water in the canal only about 40 yards. Now there is water in the whole length of the canal except the one embankment facing the rebels and this is now being undermined and will probably be blown up before long.

As you will see by the heading of this letter, the 5th N.J. Battery belongs to the 25 Corps or "Corps de Afrique" and we are in camp about 2 miles from the place where we then were, and nearer the river.

We have had several midnight alarms since that time and the battery has been moved all at once to some point or other at which an attack might be expected but we have had no fighting at all. Just as I am writing a burst of musketry has suddenly disturbed the silence of the evening. It seems to be on the left, but whether on this side of the river or the other I cannot tell. But I should not be surprised to hear the bugle call, "Boots and Saddles", at any moment. The musketry is now becoming more feeble, but even yet it sounds too strong for mere picket firing. I think the rebs have made an attack. . . .

The fighting is across the River and must be near the place where our Battery was last summer at Bermuda Hundred.

Dec 18. The firing continued at intervals all last night but everything is quiet again this morning. I believe it is Sunday today, and I cannot but regret that I am not with you to go to the chapel. There is little if any difference here between Sunday and week day, and it seems an age since I heard a hymn or a sermon.

I should like to know how the 'Sutcliffes' are getting along. I do not think you have mentioned them in any of your letters, and I tell you '*William*' is a very particular friend of mine, at least he used to be. Remember me to him if you see him and also to old *Haas*. Did he keep his word in calling to see you, when he visited Lancashire last summer?

Four of our guns are going into position in the breastworks a little way from here today. I thought we should go to North Carolina and altho' I am not certain yet whether the battery may not be ordered there, the probabilities are that we shall stay here for the winter.

I have been expecting a letter from you so long that I am almost despairing of ever getting one any more. You ought to send me a few newspapers. I like to read them. I will send you to-day's *Herald*, that is the *Herald* of the 16th for we only get a paper two days old.

P.S. *Dec 23rd 1864.* I have not heard anything more from Col. Armstrong respecting my commission in coloured troops, but I hope to hear something of it before long. I intend to write again very soon,

J.H.

5th New Jersey Battery
Before Richmond, Va.
Dec 23rd 1864

My Dear Parents,

I have just received a letter from Lt. Warren, Bro. of Capt. Warren, and addressed to the latter in which enquiries are made respecting a certain Andrew Ross who has had a college education and was a good lad, and whose mother is almost distracted by his apparent silence for over two months.

Tell my dear mother I am as right as a clock, and until this morning I have been in a constant bad humour with myself and everybody else on account of receiving no letter from you. I

112

commenced writing the third letter since receiving any from you on the 15th but I have kept waiting to hear some news of you. I enclose a portion of what I wrote.

I am downright vexed to think that my letters have been lost. The last one I sent was a letter to Sister Annie. The previous one contained a picture of the log hut I then lived in and a faithful pen and ink sketch of "Happy day, Happy land, this is a *glorious* country", and 24 pages of writing. I have been awaiting your letter with a great deal of inward cursing and swearing.

Capt. Warren has been cashiered from the service as I told you in my last and the 1st Lt. of a Rhode Island Battery commands in his place. The change seems to be none the worse for me.

To-day is Bro. William's birthday. He is twenty-five. May his happiness and prosperity be always on the increase, is the wish of his brother, James.

Day after tomorrow is Christmas, and altho' it will be 1865 when you get this (if you do have the luck to get it) you may have the consolation to know that I wished you a happy Christmas and a Merry New Year, or I should say it the other way about.

Just now I am very busy making the Clothing rolls for the Battery and after I have completed them I shall have to commence on the Muster and pay rolls.

Day after tomorrow is Christmas day and I have received an invitation to dine at headquarters. Don't be alarmed. It is only one of the clerks who has asked me to come. I do not expect a goose for dinner but we may have some slap jacks and apple dumplings. I want to send this letter off tonight in order that my mother may set her mind at rest so I will not write as long a letter as I might but, hoping in future that you will not alarm yourselves any more on my account, the mails are so irregular and insecure on this side of the Atlantic, so I remain as ever,

Your dutiful and affectionate son.

Address   Andrew Ross
5th New Jersey Battery Lt. Arty
Arty Brig: 25th A.C.
Army of the James—Va—

5th New Jersey Battery
Artillery Brigade, 25th A.C.
Army of the James, Va.
Jany 9th 1864*

My Dear Parents,

I received your ever welcome and long expected epistle with a pleasure which can only be realized by one who has been like me separated for a long time and by a most *tarnation* long distance from those he loves. I had waited so long that I almost dreaded the arrival of your letter lest it might contain the account of some disaster or misfortune to the family but instead of that:

> Good News from Home,
> Good News for me
> Has come across the deep blue sea.

And I read with gladness that all of you are well and prospering. The deaths you mention are very sorrowful, of course, but my old dad abbreviates the account in a somewhat serio-comic style by saying, So and so is dead and Owd Frank *ditto*. I have seen rather too many deaths, bloody and horrible too, for anything short of a personal visit of the grim monster, or one to some of you to affect me seriously.

I am still a private—but in less than a week I expect to be an Officer—or else know the reason why, and so soon as I do get it, of course I will let you know.

With regard to John Entwistle, I am very glad that you put him off in such a good way, but I shall not write to him or Mr Barlow until I know something worth telling, and as long as I am in the army a private, as any other *leather yed* may be, I do not think I shall ever write to a soul but to you. And again I reiterate the request that you do not tell anyone what position I hold or anything about me. I am sorry that I cannot take a commission in my own name, for reasons which must be obvious to you if you only think of the case. Suppose I told Col. Armstrong that my name was not Andrew Ross. Do you not think he would mistrust me. I know very well he would, and I should consequently miss my object. But I can tell you what I can do. After I obtain the commission I can make a confidante of Col. Armstrong and have letters addressed to me as Lieut Horrocks, care of Col. Armstrong, 8th Regt. U.S.C.I. However all this is

* He means 1865.

114

premature. I want to talk about realities and leave for a while on one side possibilities, probabilities and chimeras in general.

You know me and I know you individually and collectively. I am not afraid of you and you are not afraid of me. I have a compact set of brains which I inherited from my fat but venerable sire and rather a soft heart which I think is a leetle bit like my mothers. Very well, so far so good. And now I want to tell you something in my experience which is as true as ever I wrote in my life. Since coming into this army I have had to measure myself with other men. This is a place where everyone must stand up for himself, and if he can not do it why he must go under, and at once become victimized. Indeed the scripture proverb must be slightly changed to suit this case. "Do others or you must be done." In this school I have lived long enough to know what I am worth, and find that I am inferior to some but a very great deal superior to others, and the result of all this is that I have a position of comparative liberty while everyone else in the Battery is more or less a prisoner. I just have my work under my thumb and after disposing of it I just do as I please. I take a horse and ride over to headquarters or to the picket lines or where I please, and only mention it to the commanding officer. In fact I have a position I prefer to anything less than that of a Commissioned Officer, and I am always ready to resist any kind of imposition no matter from what source. If I cannot stand up for myself no one will stand up for me. Thank God I can do it.

Lt. Metcalf is trying to get a furlough. I could get one too but he does not wish me to be away while he is away as he fears and justly too, that everything would be topsy-turvy in the accounts of this Battery in the case of both being absent at once. But on his return, if in the meantime I do not get a commission, I am to have a furlough, and then—and then, shall I come home? No. I will tell you what I think I will do. I think I will go to Illinois and see my uncle Henry. It is *only* about a thousand miles from here, and I could go there and take stock of the folks there without making myself known unless I saw fit to do so.

Jany 12th. Lt. Metcalf and six of the men (one of whom is my bunkmate, the 1st Sergeant) have gone away on a Twenty-five days furlough this morning. When they come back I think I shall get one too, but I do not know for certain whether I will or not. I long for civilized life once more, and should very much like to go, but after all the expense would be so great that I should be as poor as a church mouse afterwards.

Jany 13th. I am writing a letter by instalments or as venerable Harry Grundy's wife would say, by extortions. Yesterday afternoon I took a ride with one of the corporals, by name O'Brien, who had obtained a special permission to be absent. I needed none.

We went up to the front near Fort Harrison to see one of our men who obtained a commission in coloured troops last winter. After seeing and having a long chat with him, O'Brien wanted to go and see a Colonel who had given him some encouragement about a commission in coloured troops. We rode over to the camp where he wanted to go and he dismounted and left his horse with me while he spoke to the Colonel. I was walking the horses back and forwards for the good of their health when four horsemen came along. I did not look particularly at them till one of them struck off and came towards me. As he approached I recognized him as *Colonel Armstrong* who so kindly encouraged me as I told you before. He came up to me and shook hands and said I thought I could not be mistaken. How do you get along etc.

We had quite a talk together before O'Brien came back. He told me that he had sent in an application for me some time ago but owing to General Butler's absence he had not received any word back in return. Also, that he was not quite sure whether or not he would be allowed more officers at present as his regiment was not half full. But told me that in a week or 10 days I must come and see him again and then if there was no chance for him to get me in his Regiment, he would introduce me to other officers of his acquaintance, and he would get me a commission in some other Regiment. I told him I would much prefer to come into his Regiment if there was any possibility of it. This just pleased him and he said that I might get a commission in some other regiment for the time being and then the very first vacancy of 1st Lieutenant that occurred in his own Regiment he would have me transferred to it.

Of course I thanked him heartily for his kindness, and he bid me goodbye and rode on with his friends. Corp. O'Brien then came up and looked rather crestfallen. He said he was afraid that his chance was pretty damned miserable, that Col. Wordsworth whom he had

116

been to see had rather thrown cold water on his hopes and aspirations. So by way of recompense I just told him the chance conversation I had had with Colonel Armstrong and I must confess that he did not seem to derive much consolation from my own good fortune compared to his.

This is the most miserable country I ever saw. It rains today. It will freeze tomorrow, the day after it will thaw and then there is mud up to one's knees everywhere.

Under such circumstances transportation is difficult. We have about 120 horses in the Battery and they received their first feed tonight for *forty-eight hours*. Poor brutes. I am sorry for them. No stable. We began to build one but the sides only are completed, and I do not know how many of them will be able to see spring after such a hard winter. Seven of them have died within a week and there are others almost unserviceable.

Tell my mother that I am in hopes of surviving this war and seeing her own loving face again. As for the box, it is in Washington at the house of one of the men in this Battery and if anything should happen to me I will have it so arranged that you shall have everything belonging to me, but such an event I humbly hope may be away somewhere in the far-off distance. It would be very poor consolation to you to get a box full of useless articles belonging to me if I was killed. So in order that such a calamity may not occur, I promise to take good care of myself—and as the Yankees say—I know how to play good points. You see I have been seventeen months in the service nearly and been in some pretty hot engagements, but never received a scratch yet. So I tell you once more. Be under no apprehensions for this child's safety. I have a presentiment that we shall see each other again, several times if not more. As for living by the sword and dying by the sword, why bless us and save us—I never hurt a fly with my sword yet. The most I did in the way of hurting anybody was to fire off a few charges of canister and case shot amongst the Johnnys, ie the Rebels, and I only did that in fun. I meant no harm by it. I only pulled a string—and the thing went bang. Was I to blame for that? Why—of course not. Look at the old Duke of Wellington. He lived to a good old age and then died in a nice armchair without any sword about him at all. Buonaparte died in bed. What more encouragement does anybody want. That's what I want to know, and that's what's the matter.

My dad's a good old cock. He says, Go in and win my lad. Well of course I am just going to. But keep all your hats on. Don't get excited but exercise a little fortitude. Perseverance and a little sweet oil works wonders.

Gruber does very well to say tell him to make his fortune directly. Why the devil don't *he* do it? Fortunes are just as hard to make here as anywhere else, I believe.

However it shows his good feeling and tell him I send my regards to him as I think he is a Gentleman in spirit every inch of him.

This morning before I got up I laughed till the bunk shook. George Fisher, the first duty Sergeant, having stepped into the 1st Sergeant's shoes while he is away, came into my house (log hut) and slept with me. He is a first class soldier and a first rate fellow and when he tries to be funny he minces his words, that is talks in an extra refined manner. This morning he woke me up about ½ past 3 o.c. and said, "*Mister Ross*, oh *do* excuse me I *beg*, for waking you up so early, but I feel so cold myself that I *really* should like to know if you do not feel the same sensation." I acknowledged it. So he says, "Well in that case we must really have a fire. *I* should be perfectly willing to freeze to death myself for the good of the country but we cannot do without *you* yet." Then he bellowed out, "Guard. Guard. Sentry. Sentry." So the sentry came and George said, "Why in Hell don't you hurry up when I call? Ah, don't say a word. Sleeping on post, no doubt. Court Martial. To be shot to death with musketry and all that sort of thing. Now if you want to get off this time, just go and wake up "Clawson" and tell him to come to me immediately."

By and by Clawson came, and George made him build a fire. When the fire was burning cheerfully, George said, "Clawson you are a fine boy. I greatly admire you, and *Mister Clawson*, you must really forgive me for disturbing your slumbers so very early, but the fact is you see it is a case of necessity. Mister Ross has been taken very sick during the night. He has vomited very considerably, and (confidentially) *Mister* Clawson, I pissed in bed through anxiety and fright. . . . Thankyou Clawson. Put a few more sticks of wood on the fire and then go and creep into bed again, that's a good boy."

You say that Annie is a Bobby dazzler and that Walter is a fine boy. I am glad to hear it, and I shall not forget them nor Bendigo, nor Pether. Bro. William's success cheers me up. It is the most complete victory of science and intrinsic worth over ignorance and punyism that ever I knew. I should very much like to have his picture, and a letter from him. Also tell eawr Jody un Henry to write to me.

If George has come home and you want to make him laugh, just tell him about the way I once made him laugh, after I had made him cry once a long time ago.

And now in conclusion I will say, God Bless You, God Bless Miss Mort, and God bless Owd Maria.

Eh Mesther Horrox pratin i't streets did yo say.

Your own loving Son
James

5th New Jersey Battery
Artillery Brigade 25th A.C.
Before Richmond, Va.
February 2nd 1865

My Dear Father and Mother,

I have just received your letter dated January 7th and read it with great pleasure. I also got two newspapers, the *Chronicle* and the *Farnworth Observer*, for which I thank you very sincerely. I should like you to send me the *London Times*.

Tell my sister Annie that I have been expecting a letter from her for some time with her "Carte de Visite" and also Miss Mort's and as many other pretty ones as she can get. I hope she will not keep me waiting much longer.

I am sorry that I am as yet disappointed in getting a commission. I took a ride over to Col. Armstrong's Regiment a few days ago and had a chat with him. He said he could not get officers for his Regiment. He has had five vacancies for some time and has made application several times to have me appointed to one of them, but since General Butler's removal, there has been only a few solitary appointments made. But Col. Armstrong still gives me much encouragement and said amongst other things, "A man of your intelligence is safe to get a commission if he desires it."

Lt. Warren (Captain Warren's brother) is now in command of the battery during the absence of Lt. Metcalf. He said to me last night, "Ross, if I were you I would not go in the coloured troops." I asked him why not. "Well," he said, "you are more comfortable here than

119

you will be with picket duty to do, guard duty and every other disagreeable thing." "Yes Lieutenant," said I. "You are quite right in what you say, but I have a little *too much ambition to be content to remain as a private.*" "Well," he said, "I like you for that, but you wait a little and something better may turn up for you."

A few nights ago, we had a few real nigger minstrels playing and singing for us, and dancing too. The songs are some I have never heard before, and do not bear the slightest resemblance to the songs sung by the burnt cork imitations I have heard both in New York and England. One of them related the story of the rich man and Lazarus. It was sung very sweetly by a burly woolly-headed negro, who played a very pretty accompaniment on the banjo. I can only remember a few words of it. The rich man, according to the words of the song, lived in a city called Jerusaloram,

> The poor man died
> And went to Abram's buzzoram.
> Glory to the Lamb,
> Glory Hallilujoram etc, etc.

Another song which I have no doubt was the composition of some negro was called, Babylon is Fallen, Babylon being only the type of the Institution of Slavery. The refrain of each verse was,

> Look out now
> For I am going to shoot.
> Babylon is fallen
> And we're gwine to occupy the land.

It was very well sung and I enjoyed it amazingly. An Irishman who danced a hornpipe was the life and soul of the party. I laughed till my sides ached at the marvellous capers he cut. His arms, legs, head and body all were going together keeping good time to the music, and every now and then he would scream out, "Och, Biddy me darlint. I'd die for yez. Hide nothin. Bi the powers of Maul Kelly's Cat, and that's no fool of an oath, we'll all be in Richmond soon. Bean soup tomorrow for dinner and no work. That's me. Ock Batherashin." etc, etc.

I cannot imagine what the effect would have been if I had stood up and proposed that we, the Irishman, niggers and all included, should join in a few words of prayer. My dear dad, you ask me if I could not get up a little religious service once every sabbath. In answer I must say that such a thing would be considered by the men of this Battery as the best joke of the season. It would be literally *casting pearls before swine.*

There are very strong rumors of peace afloat. Of course you have heard of Blair's Mission to Richmond. I heard from good authority today that Stevens, the Vice-President of the Confederate States, came through our lines today to go to Washington with the object of negotiating peace. There has been a bet made between two of our men that we shall have peace in 15 days, and I know many who are ready to wager that we shall have peace inside of six months. Won't there be a jubilanto in this country if peace be made. I think you will wish to be here to see it.

Two or three of the men want me to go with them home when the war is over and promise to give me a good time of it. One of them says I must have his sister, who he guarantees to be a real smart gal. . . . No thank you. I am not matrimonially inclined just at present, unless there is a real smart heap of a dowry to come with the dowdy.

You must have had a good time of it at Edgeworth the day after New Year's. I think we must regard Brother William as a flourishing fixture of that locality.

I am rather sorry to hear of W. & A. Openshaw losing a law suit. Things like these are generally rather expensive and have been known to bring down many a firm with a crash, to lots of shillings in the pound.

I hope by this time that Bro. George has returned to you safe and sound.

Look here Bro. Peter, dost thou see any resemblance here in this picture . . . to a little lad who used to shoot marbles so well? No, you don't. Me neither. All right. You see he is learning his lessons. Go and do likewise.

There is no news of any interest that I can tell you. Only what you have no doubt already read in the English papers.

I hope this cruel war will soon be over. I think there is every probability of it; and then, what then? I don't know yet. I often think how nice it would be to be at home once more. I do not know whether I could play on the piano very well or not. It is so long since I tried. But I think we could have a few merry nights together. But I

121

think I shall defer that pleasure till I have some money to back me out against *all creation.*

> Gold Gold Gold Gold,
> Heavy to get but light to hold,
> How unduly its agencies vary
> To raise, to ruin, to curse, to bless
> As even its minted coins express
> Now stamped with the image of good Queen Bess
> And now of a bloody Mary.

You must think I am hard up for stuff to make a letter with when I am obliged to go quoting poetry.

There is one thing I have left out that I must mention. I am very sorry for the many bereavements of my Uncle James, my pompous but very unfortunate namesake. I tell you what, father. I do not think you ever suffered the same kind of poverty he has suffered. While he used to be trying to live in state, the poor old man was as poor as a church-mouse. I know Mason well and am glad if he is doing well for himself and my Uncle James too.

If you see Coz. Rachel give her my love and sympathies. I'll be blowed if I like anyone outside our own family better than I do her. Also tell William Sutcliffe, my old friend, that I have not forgot him by no manner of means. Tell him I am in a first rate state of health and spirits and hope he is the same. Have you heard from old Haas lately? Tell me all about him when you write.

I enclose a picture of Little Red Ridinghood for Bro. Ben.

There are a great many deserters come into our lines every day.

I must now conclude. With love to all, believe me to be

Affectionately yours
James Horrocks

> 5th New Jersey Battery Lt. Arty.
> Arty Brig. 25th A.C.
> Army of the James, Va.
> Feby 23rd 1865

My Dear Parents,

I am well and hearty and sincerely hope that you and all our family are the same. I have been expecting a letter from you for some days past, but have been disappointed. Perhaps the reason is because you have no news to tell. In that case you ought at least to write and tell me so. I cannot tell you how long it seems to wait for your letters. They seem to come so seldom.

I have a few items of news to tell you. First and foremost Captain Warren has come back and again taken command of the Battery and the first written order he gave to the Battery was the following,

> Before Richmond, Va.
> Feby 18th 1865

Company Orders, No.1. New Series.
1. Quartermaster Sergt. Nicholas Relinger is hereby reduced to the rank of Sergt.
2. Private Andrew Ross is hereby promoted to the rank of Quartermaster Sergt. and all other non-commissioned officers and privates will obey and respect him accordingly.

I need scarcely say that the above was a very pleasant surprise for me, and I must also say that all the men of the Battery with a few envious and contemptible exceptions, seemed glad and congratulated me on my newly acquired dignity. I now wear scarlet stripes an inch and a half wide on my pants and chevrons on my jacket. My pay is 24 dollars a month I think but am not quite sure.

Of course I am very thankful to Capt. Warren for his favor. But after all you must remember, I stood by him when he was in trouble, and did all I could for him to save him from dismissal, and when I saw clearly that he was sure to be dismissed even if he should not get something worse I advised him to resign, and raise a new Battery and make me 1st Lieutenant. But he thought he could get over it, and got dismissed after all. And even then I took the trouble to write a long letter for him to General Butler (You know I can write a good one sometimes) showing forth the mitigating circumstances in his case. He seems to have had a great deal more influence than I thought he had and has managed to get reinstated. Well he did not forget me, but the first thing he did was to write the order before mentioned and have it read out to the men on parade.

I like the position very well. Yesterday I rode down to the landing on the James River and drew a supply of clothing for the Battery and issued it today. Tomorrow I am going to try and draw about twenty horses, as we have lost a good many the last two months through exposure and scanty food.

It is my duty to see about all the rations of the men and forage for the horses, and to take charge of the property of the Battery generally. The Captain is held responsible for it and the Quartermaster Sergeant is the keeper, or I may say acts as the Captain's agent in charge.

I am still living in the same house with the Orderly Sergeant. We two have a house to ourselves (log shanty). The rest of the men live 16 in a house.

The day Captain Warren came to the Battery, Lieutenant Edwin Chappell left with a twenty days' leave of absence.

He called me into his house before he left and told me that he intended to resign his commission as soon as he got to Washington, and then he should start for England. (He is an Englishman.) I told him if he liked to call on my folks they would be glad to see him and he could tell them all about Virginia etc. He said he would call and see you if it cost him five pounds. I gave him Bro. William's address and informed him that I was in the army under an assumed name. I dare say he will call at Bro. Williams and he can bring him over to see you. His home is in Devon.

Rebels are deserting and coming into our lines very rapidly. I met 43 of them yesterday going down to the boat to be shipped North. I think this war will be over very soon, and then we shall have a gay old time.

The latest news I hear is that Charleston is evacuated and Fort Anderson, opposite to Wilmington, taken by our troops. What do you think of the Confederacy—caving in very rapidly, or I may say collapsing like red hot flues.

My dear Parents, I am as right as a clock, or ninepence. (Ninepence might be wrong though if you offered it in payment for two sixpenny pittle pots. Shakespeare.)

I am just going to bed. God bless you all. I will write more tomorrow morning.

Feb 24th. There have been no steps taken as yet with regard to my commission. But I have not given up the idea yet altho' I do not care so much about it now as when I was a private. There are several things more advantageous in my present position than in the coloured troops. For instance the duties are not so arduous. There is no picket or guard duty, and above all I have no trudging through the mud. When I go, I go mounted like a gay cavalier ought to go. The only reason I want to go into the "Black Brigade" is ambition.

Before Richmond, Va.
Feby 25th 1865

My Dear Widowed Mother,

I have read Bro. Joseph's letter bearing the ill tidings and have been weeping ever since. Oh my heart aches for you, my poor mother. It is a great blow to me, and I cannot think what the effect will be on one who has been the partner in weal and woe for so many years, of him who is now in a better land. Yes, he is in heaven. If there is a certainty of a happy future for anyone, it must surely be for him whose heart was always in his duty, who loved as but few love, and whose greatest joy was in promoting the happiness of others. Try to bear it dear mother with Christian fortitude. Do not fret. Remember you have many loving children to share your woe.

And I will not stay away from you any longer than I can help. I will come mother dear, and share your sorrow, and if possible I will be with you before long. But oh! I think of my dear father. All his children were with him but me. I would have liked to have seen his smiling face once again but, God's will be done. My day dreams have been all about a happy return home, and every little thing that was funny, I treasured it up in my memory, thinking how it would make my father laugh. My dreams are over. I come back to the sad reality of our loss. It is heavy and as yet I cannot see anything but the dark side of the picture. I pray I may be enabled to see God's hand in it—for I am miserable.

My heart was light this morning but it is very heavy now. I think I ought to be at home, striving to make my father's loss more bearable to you. He always provided well for his children, and now they are orphans, each one must do his best for the others. Let us each one try to make each other happy.

I enclose a letter that I was writing before the bad news came.

God bless you all, is the fervent prayer of yours, in mourning,

James Horrocks

5th New Jersey Battery
Arty. Brig 25th A.C.
March 10th 1865

My Dear Mother,

I wrote a letter to you about ten days ago, and have since received the newspapers containing the account of my dear father's death. I should very much like to come home but I am afraid it will be almost impossible for me to do so at present.

Three days ago I was summoned before a board of examiners to pass the ordeal for a commission in colored troops, and after the examination Colonel Armstrong, who was one of the board, came out and, putting his hand on my shoulder, said, "I congratulate you. You have passed very well and very easily." I thanked him and asked him how soon I should receive the appointment. He said he could scarcely tell me, but I might depend upon it before long.

If I take this appointment I can resign in six months, but not before, as the War Department will not accept a resignation under any circumstances before an officer has been six months mustered in, the reason of this being that many take this method of getting out of the service.

But in the meantime I shall be getting about $130.00 a month with which I shall have to support myself and servant. I think I can save at least $50.00 a month of this after I have bought and paid for my first outfit. This you know will be better than a situation in England where I do not believe I could get a pound a week.

I expect by the time you get this I shall have the shoulder straps on, but, I wish you to direct your letters as before to:

Q.M. Sergt. Andrew Ross
5th New Jersey Battery
Arty Brig. 25th A.C.
Army of the James, Va.
U.S. of America

as I shall be able to get them just the same, whether I am in the Battery or not.

I am in very good health. Indeed I think I was never better in my life but for the cloud that has come over our family so suddenly. I should be happy enough. But the sad news of the loss of my dear father has grieved me to the heart. It is so sad to think I shall never see him again. But fretting and lamentations are in vain. He has gone to a better land where we may meet him at last.

> In heaven above where all is love
> There will be no more sorrow there.

It is rainy, muddy and cold here at present. The roads are in awful condition. The guns of the Battery are in position in the breast-works, two in Fort Burnham, two in a fort to the left and two near Fort Brady. The caissons and horses are in this camp with the Captain, Orderly Sergeant and myself and about 70 men (drivers and artificers etc). I have very little work to do, good quarters and middling good grub.

Last night I was called into the Captain's quarters to look over the list of property turned over by Lt. Metcalf when the Captain took command. It seems that the captain had receipted for more sabres than he intended to, and Lieutenant Maxwell was telling him that a trick had been played him in having the figures altered.

He said, "You must keep your eyes open when you are dealing with a Yankee." (Maxwell is an Englishman.) "I would not trust one of them the breadth of my finger."

"Why," said the Captain, "I am a Yankee, Lieutenant."

"Well," said Maxwell, "I wouldn't trust them by G——."

I could not help laughing and the Captain too.

I have no news of importance so you must excuse the shortness of my letter. Write as soon as you can.

Hoping you are all well.

I remain dutifully yours
James Horrocks

> 114 Cedar Street
> New York City
> March 29th '65

My Very Dear Mother,

As you see by the heading of this I am in New York. I came here on furlough on the 16th inst. and am to be back again to the Battery on the 5th April 65, so I shall start for Washington on Saturday the 1st April.

You will very likely ask why I do not come home. The reason is this. Unfortunately I could not get my pay when I started from the front. If I had I should have left everything and come home to you. Oh how I should have liked to do so, but it was impossible. I had not money enough. I tried to ship as ordinary seaman on the same vessel that Lieut. Chappell is on. (He is 2nd Mate.) He wanted me to come along with him very much and I had made up my mind to do so when lo! Behold! when I went down to the Shipping Office I found that the Complement was filled and I could not go. So I think it will be my best policy to return to the Army. There I am sure of a Lieutenant's Commission and in a few months' time I shall be able to resign and come home honorably, and besides that there is about $100 pay due me, which will go a long way to pay for an outfit.

Depend upon it, I shall come home yet. Do not fret yourself about me at all. Remember, I love you and if there was no other tie to bind me, that alone is enough to prevent me doing anything reckless or improvident. I hope Bro. Henry is doing well for you, but I am afraid now that dear father is gone, his creditors may come down on the property like a thousand of bricks or Mr Himners may sell the property which there is no denying has been a very poor investment. But never mind, Mother. You have several sons who will never see you want for anything. I myself have been a very slender reed for you to lean on but—live in hopes. I shall come up to time yet, and be as good as a son to you.

I hope Sister Annie, and Bros. Walter, Peter and Benjamin are as good and clever as they ought to be. For the Rest I have no fears. Give my love to all, and to Miss Mort. Kind remembrances to William Sutcliffe and to Old Haas if you hear from them or see them.

The Southern Confederacy may hold out some time yet but they can never bring the same force into the field as formerly. They are losing ground all the time, and at no great while they must cave in.

I need not tell you the war news. You read that in the English papers every day.

Sergeant Archer of our Battery called to see me the other day and we went together to a place called Tremont. (Sergt. Archer is on furlough.) There there was a pigeon shooting match and Sergt. Archer competed with a lot of sporting gents for a double-barrelled gun worth 40 dollars. There was not birds enough to decide the battle, and the prize lay between three of them. Sergt. Archer, I am proud to say being one of the three, he sold his chance to the other two for $8.

I will write again before long. For the present believe me as ever,

Your very affectionate
James   *Address as before.*

5th New Jersey Battery
Arty. Brig. 25th A.C.
Richmond, Va.
April 8th 1865

My Dear Bro. Joseph,

I was in New York when your letter dated March 3rd arrived at the Battery, and I therefore did not receive it till the 6th inst, when I came back to the Battery. To day I received Bro. William's letter dated March 14th. I need scarcely say that I read both letters with much pleasure and a little pain. I was sorry to learn that Bro. George is not quite up to the mark, but it is only what might be expected. A seafaring life is brutalizing in its effect and I think a man must have a very superior order of intellect, who after years spent on board a ship, is either more intelligent or more fit for civilized society than he was previously. One point I must mention before I go further, you say that if business in the mill is more prosperous you think you will throw up your present position, and enter with Henry. I honestly think you can make money, especially if you had a fair start, in *any business*, but to begin with an incubus of debt, I think is not only unfair, but it incurs annoyance, trouble, vexation of spirit, and a constant burden. Now I know pretty well how the case stands. There is a bill of sale on the property for an amount that the whole concern would scarcely fetch in the market today. There are creditors who can pounce down at any moment they think proper. I do not think they will, only they can. Now my advice is let the thing be settled in a court of bankruptcy. The creditors have received one third of their dues already and I think they will be very apt to let the thing be considered settled and when you can thus begin clear I would rent the mill from Mr Hinmers or whoever had it if I could do so at a moderate sum.

I do not know but that I am rather presumptuous in thus offering advice gratis, but of course you will forgive me and let me add that I have full and perfect confidence to trust you in doing what is best for my dear mother and the family. I think you did the right thing when you gave George to understand that in future he will have to look to himself for outfits and everything else.

My Bro. William's account of the woman who lived 12 weeks on the diet of a fish is startling and worthy a record in the *Lancet*. I suppose Sister Annie sent me the Carte de Visite of Miss Hartley. It is very good. I think she is a lovely girl.

I left New York last Sunday evening and arrived in Washington the next morning. I was walking along Seventh St in Washington and saw a crowd gathering in front of the War Department. I hastened up to see the cause and a gentleman was standing on the top of the stone steps making a speech. I was informed that this was Andrew Johnson, the Vice Prest. of the U.S. The first words I heard him utter were, "Richmond is ours . . . and the rebel army in full retreat with Grant in pursuit." And then Oh! the cheering, the howling, the waving of handkerchiefs and hats. It was tremendous.

I heard also that the 25th A.C. was the first to enter the city, so I knew that the 5th N.J. Battery must be *in Richmond*. I will not dwell on the excitement etc in Washington but describe my own experience as briefly as possible.

I left Washington on Tuesday and arrived at Varina landing on the James River about 4 o'clock the next day. I had a valise with me that was pretty heavy and did not feel inclined for a walk of 11 or 12 miles if I could ride. So I waited till a waggon came across the pontoon bridge. I asked the driver who was a darkey if he was going to Richmond. He said Yes, but that I could not ride as he had a very heavy load. I looked and found he was telling me the truth so I told him that I would put my valise in the waggon and walk alongside. This he at first refused but a gentle hint from me to the effect that I would pull him down and tear him *limb from limb* if he attempted to prevent me, cooled him down a little and we were soon on our way to this city. An old negress with a dress that was tattered and torn and a look that was all forlorn, crinoline all forsworn and a horrible squint that she must have had when she was born, trudged along with us. (Excuse the rhyme and the want of rhythm. It is the best I can do on such a subject.) We passed our line of works and came to those of the rebels and I had an opportunity of seeing the preparations Lee had made for Grant should he have attempted to take the city by storm. They were the most complete I ever saw, but it was dark before we arrived at Richmond. At least, it was not daylight but fortunately there was a pretty good moon. The city I found to be partially destroyed, as you will probably have learnt by the papers before you read this. There is however enough of it left to make it quite a city. I made enquiries and could learn no tidings of the 5th New Jersey Battery so I then inquired for, and at length found, Gen. Weitzell's Headquarters.

There I made enquiries for the Battery and, finding that it was about 2 miles away in some direction, I willingly accepted the sentinel's invitation to stay the night. So I lay down and slept on the floor of a room till morning. This happened to be the former residence of Jeff Davis, so lately indeed as Sunday last. So I had the honor of sleeping in the house of Jeff Davis if there is any honor in that.

The next morning I set out for the Battery and had not proceeded far when I met one of our men, who piloted me to the spot where I am now writing. All the boys were glad to see me. So was the Captain. He gave me a drink of Rebel whiskey in honor of my return. (It was bad liquor tho'.)

April 10th. The latest news this morning is that Lee has surrendered himself to Grant with his whole army. The war is virtually over, and I have not the least doubt but that in a month from now we shall be discharged. I am not at all anxious under these circumstances to obtain the commission I expected to get. That regiment is with a portion of the 25th A.C. with Grant. They went to the Southside railroad and are probably in the direction of Lynchburg.

The Colonel was down to the Battery twice while I was on furlough and seemed much disappointed that he could not see me.

I should be very glad to come home again even if it was only for a day or two, just to see you all. But I cannot do it just yet, so I will send you with this my photograph, that I had taken in New York. I also enclose one for Miss Mort. I hope you will like them. They are considered pretty good.

I also enclose two Confederate bills. I suppose I can get a few thousand dollars for one *greenback*. It is of no value now and I suppose it never will be again.

The Battery has gone on picket this morning about 4 o'clock. I am still left in the camp with charge of the spare horses and sufficient number of men to look after and guard them.

I went into the city this morning and got acquainted with two or three families. They express themselves very well satisfied with the change, only they have no money but confederate and consequently are rather hard put to it to procure food and the necessaries of life.

I notice one thing in Richmond. The miscegenation of races. Some are as black as the ace of spades and there is every shade of colour to be seen in the streets from that to a perfect Circassian complexion. One young lady in particular was pointed out to me who, altho' she was as white as I am (if not a little more so for I am rather tanned), and who has the education of a lady, was never free until the day our troops came into Richmond, and she is living with her old master yet. I suppose she has been to all intents and purposes free, and consequently she does not realize the difference.

I will now conclude. Address as before.

Give my love to Miss Mort and all enquiring friends and accept all of you the heartfelt affection of,

Your affectionate brother
James

5th New Jersey Battery
Arty Brig. 25th A.C.
Nr. Petersburg, Va.
April 19th 1865

My Dear Brother William,

I received your letter in Richmond as I intimated in the epistle to Brother Joseph and I need not tell you how much pleasure it gave me to read it. As you have probably by this time read full particulars of the fall of Richmond, the surrender of General Lee and the assassination of Abe. Lincoln, I need not enter into particulars. Events come thick and fast, and I hope that the next great event will be my discharge from the service. Such a small affair will not probably cause much of a sensation in the world, but it will be of infinitely more importance *to me* than these great affairs of nations, and then my boy you may look out through that window of yours that overlooks the valley etc, so soon to be metamorphosed into an inland little sea, for a poor miserable wretch to come along dusty, tired and forlorn. You will see him approach nearer and nearer until you recognize in his pale visage a resemblance to your long lost brother Jamie. Then throw open the massive portals of your palatial mansion. Clasp him to your breast and with tears in your eyes, give utterance to your wishes: "Jimmie, my lad, you shall live with me, eat at the same table with me, ride in my carriage with me, and tha knows, b-b-black my boots. . . ." Don't that put you in mind of my dear old dad. Oh I tell you I can remember such a lot of things that he used to say in his peculiar manner, but alas! we have heard them for the last time. We shall never see or hear him again. And as Hamlet says, "He was a man. Take him for all in all, we ne'er shall see his like again." And my dear mother, how does she bear it? I hope it is with Christian resignation. Oh! I tell you, if anything should happen to her and I should never see her again, I think my heart would break. I should feel miserable on her account if I did not know that all of you love her just as much as I do and will do everything that can be done to make her happy.

I am very sorry that your horse has been sick and hope that the little operation you made will have caused his entire recovery.

I was riding at a gallop through the streets of Richmond a few days before we left, and turning a corner my little horse slipped and fell heavily. I luckily fell on my feet catlike and tried to raise my fallen charger, but the poor brute seemed stunned and made no effort to raise himself and very soon I had a whole crowd around me, black and white, commiserating me and *poor Bill*. Many of them came forward to assist me, but I just delicately informed them all that I required no assistance and wanted no pity at all and when my little pony seemed to come round to himself I just took the bridle rein in one hand and patting his neck with the other I addressed him in a language not to be found in any dictionary but which he fully understood and he just made one spring and landed safely on his four understandings, gave himself one shake and then pawed the ground knowingly. He rose so suddenly that two or three darkies who were rather closer than prudence would suggest exercised considerable agility in getting clear, so much indeed that two of them fell on their latter end bringing down two or three others in the vain attempt to retain their equilibrium. I smiled, then vaulted into the saddle like a son of Mars, gave one supercilious look at the crowd below, touched Billy's flanks with my Mexican spurs and went on my way rejoicing in right gallant style.

We were ordered to march from Richmond about a week ago, and came down here which is a place about four miles south of Petersburg. The reason of our *exodus* from Richmond is currently stated to be on account of the niggers. To a people who have kept the negro in his proper place, it was especially galling to see them in the uniform of the United States and be obliged to submit to their impertinence and insults. Many complaints were made to the General in Command and at length we got the order to leave with the "Corps de Afrique" and here we are in a place that has been overrun by Grant's army so I need not tell you it is completely desolate. We have however good quarters, good stables and good water left behind by the aforesaid army. I am tired of the place already and do not care how soon I go to some other for a change. It is very probable that we shall move soon. Indeed there is a rumor that we shall be on the march tomorrow but in what direction the Lord only knows. I should be glad if it proved to be for Washington, preparatory to the muster out of service, but I am afraid no such luck will be ours. I will now leave off writing and go to bed. It is rather hard—being composed of shingles—and only one blanket between those and your body but I can sleep there comfortably and serenely. I wish to heaven I may never have a worse couch. Then good night my bully boy till the morrow.

April 20th. The startling news has just come that Gen. Grant has also been assassinated. If this state of things continue the people of this country will begin to see how much better is a monarchy like our own than a republic.

April 30th. Excuse the long gap between this and the last line I wrote. The rumor of Grant's assassination is false as you are probably aware before you read this. However to leave these little matters on one side and proceed to the big ones, namely, those relating to my own self individually and collectively. We have been on the march since I left off on the 20th and are now on the banks of the Appomattox, a few miles above Petersburg. Tonight I received a letter from Brother Henry, and read it with a great deal of pleasure. There is very little of it to reply to, altho' it is very interesting. When anyone tells you news and does not ask you any questions, all you can do is just tell him what you think of it and tell him your own news in return, or else if you happen to feel *pugnacious* you may politely inform him that he is a *d—d liar*. However I will not do anything of the kind to my dear Bro. Henry, and as no comments are necessary, save one, that he has greatly improved in his handwriting since he last wrote to me, and his signature is very much like Bro. Joseph's, (That is a compliment, I assure you). I will proceed to unfold my narrative, as the monkey said when he jumped down the tree.

There is good news in the paper today regarding the speedy disbanding of the volunteer troops. Everything seems to indicate that we shall be free men in less than a month. If I receive all the bounty and pay that is due me, I shall have about $*200.00* to do as I like with. I have not quite made up my mind what I shall do and would like if possible to just ask your advice. But most probably I shall be obliged to exercise my own judgement in the matter. You may perhaps feel some curiosity about what course I intend to pursue. If when I get to New York a good opportunity comes under my notice I think I shall take it. But if not I shall cross the Briny Ocean once more and come home to see you all. As to that little brat which caused such a sensation a couple of years ago, I never intend to pay a damned halfpenny to keep it, and I do not think I shall come home *to stay*. If I come at all it will only be for a very short time and that will be secret.

Col. Armstrong is now Brevet Brig. General. I saw him about ten days ago and he expressed himself very much surprised at the long delay in my commission. He told me that my recommendation had been sent in by the board of examiners to Gen. Weitzell who had approved it and forwarded it to the War Department for action.

That is the last of it I think. But I assure you I should very much prefer my discharge from the army than any commission that can be offered to me.

I am rejoiced to think how well you are all doing, and I have a very great longing to come home and just see you all and talk things over.

I have very good times in the Battery at present. As Quartermaster Sergeant I have a free pass to go and come whenever I please. I have a man to take care of my horse etc. His name is William Gibbon. I think he would do almost anything for me. He washes for me, cleans my sabre, belt and spurs, and horse equipment, saddles my horse for me when I go anywhere and unsaddles him when I return. In short he is what the fellows here call my *dog-robber*. Such a title is rather curious. I believe that origin of it is this: If an officer has such a man, he generally allows him to dine from the leavings on the table, so as the man gets what is the dog's share, he is called a dog-robber.

May 1st 1865. The day is very gloomy. I think we shall have rain before long. We have had some very pleasant weather here lately. I will leave off writing now as I have got nothing else to talk about but the weather and I do not think I shall post this letter till tomorrow as I expect some stamps from Washington tonight that I sent for about a week ago.

I cannot buy twenty-four cent stamps here and I hate to send it without stamp. By the way I had to send for Bro. Henry's letter to Fortress Monroe, as I received a notice that there was a letter to my address at the P.O. there, due 69 cents. I sent 70 cents for it and received it, as I told you, last night. The letter had a shilling stamp on it and was no heavier than many a one that has come from you for the same. I think the Post Master at Fortress Monroe is a G—d—d swindler and I have a good mind to write and tell him so.

May 5th 1865. Since writing the above the Battery has moved from the banks of the Appomattox to the Banks of the James, a couple of miles below City Point. There is every probability that our next move will be to Washington and then to New Jersey to be mustered out of the service.

So I think that it will be better to address your next letter to:
James Horrocks
Post Office
New York City, N.Y.
To be left till called for.

I will now conclude with love to all of you, Miss Mort included, remaining ever,

Your affectionate brother
James

May 29th 1865

My Dear Mother,
    I am in first rate health and spirits and hope sincerely you and all the family are the same.
    Since writing my last, several things of importance have occurred in my own career.
    On the 24th I received a Commission from the President of the United States, as 2nd Lieutenant in the 8th U.S.C.I. I could have refused to take it but as there was no certainty as to the time of the discharge of the Battery from the service, I considered it much better to accept the appointment. I therefore reported for duty to Brevet Brig. Gen. Armstrong the same evening and he welcomed me very cordially. He said I told you I would have you in my regiment and, altho' I have been a long time getting it, it has come at last. He then informed me that the regiment would embark for *Texas* the following day and he wished me to push forward with my discharge papers etc and be ready to go with the regiment the following day.
    At 4 o'clock p.m. on the 24th inst. I was in the ordinary discharge of my duty at the 5th N.J. Battery without a thought or hope of anything more than ordinary except perhaps a speedy discharge from the army with the whole Battery. Twenty-four hours from that time, I had been discharged from the army, mustered into it again as an officer, bid goodbye to Capt. Warren, and was on a steamboat going down the James River.
    When we arrived at Fortress Monroe, we went from the River-boat to an Ocean steamer, the *Illinois*. The 8th Regiment is the only one on board but General Jackson and his staff are also on board. It is the finest vessel in the fleet and the reason the 8th is along with the Commanding Officer of the division is because it has the best band in the Corps.
    Of course the officers have all state rooms. I have the honor of breakfasting, dining and supping with Brig. General Jackson, Brevet Brigadier General Armstrong and a number of other officers of high rank.
    I went on shore day before yesterday to try and get my pay at Fortress Monroe. I was unable to get it, but while there I was conversing with the Officer of the Guard at Fortress Monroe, who

told me that Jeff Davis (now confined in a casemate in the fort) seemed very dejected. Shackles were put on his legs the other day. Jeff resisted and he had to be thrown on his back and it took six men to put the irons on him. I am afraid he will be hung.

The next day I went down to Norfolk, the Headquarters of the Paymaster's department, and after some trouble and a great deal of annoyance I was paid. On my final statements, according to my calculation, I ought to have had pay amounting to $153, allowance for clothing $10, and I was not quite sure that I would not get the $75 balance of bounty that is due me. But instead of that, I was only allowed $4½ for clothing, and instead of receiving the extra $75, I had to pay back the advance bounty of the United States $25. Consequently I only received $131½. With this sum I bought a few of the most necessary articles of my outfit, and have still enough money to pay my way for a while. My pay will now be about $140 dollars a month, with which I shall have to support myself and servant. The officers of the regiment seem to be perfect gentlemen so far as I have seen anything of them. The sensation is decidedly funny when you have been accustomed to salute an officer in uniform, when you meet one, to suddenly find yourself put on a level with them and entitled to all the deference, respect and obedience that formerly you yielded instead of exacted.

Mother, I am now a gentleman in everything but money and I may overcome that drawback in time.

You need not tell anyone where I am as they would probably wish to write to me and I do not care that anyone should know I was living under an assumed name. The only thing would be if anyone is very importunate in wanting to know my address and you do not want to refuse it, give it as to James Horrocks, care of Lieut. Andrew Ross etc and explain the reason of address that way how you think best.

You might say that I was on the move all the time and that to address it care of Lieut. Andrew Ross was the safest way for me to get it. However I do not want anyone to write to me at all, only you, but if there is any necessity for it the aforementioned plan of addressing I judge to be the best.

Since writing to Brother William I have not received any letter from any of you but did receive a newspaper, or rather the London *Punch* from Bro. Joseph, for which I thank him. But I want you to write as often as possible.

The cabin in which I am writing is the most gorgeous and luxurious that ever I saw. The brass band is playing on the deck, and all the sights and sounds around me are so much in contrast to what I experienced a short week ago that it is almost as if I had suddenly left the hard realities of life and been transported to Fairyland.

There will probably be little or on fighting down in Texas. Kirby Smith is the only one holding out against the Federal forces and the probability is that he will cave in before we get down there.

I must now conclude. My love to all the family and to Miss Mort. Kind recollections to everybody who asks about me, especially Mr Barlow, Mr Spe and Mr John Entwistle.

Write as often as possible. If I am in urgent need of coming home I can come, if I resigned. The resignation might not be accepted but I could commit myself someway so I should be dismissed from the service.

Au revoir
James Horrocks

Camp 8th U.S.C.T. Infy.
Brazos de Santiago, Texas
June 22nd 1865

My Dear Mother and Sister and Brothers,

It is some time since I wrote to you. My last letter was sent from Fortress Monroe and was dated about May 29th. If you received it, which I hope you did, you are already aware that your unworthy relative, myself, is now a *Lieutenant* in the United States Service. I am in good health and comfortably situated and that is about as much happiness as generally falls to the lot of us humans. If I could only *see and talk with you* for a while, the measure of my joy would be about complete; but as I cannot do that, the next best thing is to receive your letters, and it becomes my painful but very imperative duty while on that point, to remark *en passant* that it is, as near as I can tell, *two months* since I heard from you, and that it was Brother Henry's letter, the first one he wrote to me since leaving the blessed dominion of Victoria Regina—The land of my birth, The land of the free, So it ever shall be; Yes the happiest land upon earth.

Perhaps one reason why it is so long a time is on account of my recent grand change of base: it is four weeks since I left the Battery, and have been on the move ever since till within a few days ago, when I arrived with the rest of the "Eighth" at this place or rather I ought to say at the island of Padre which is across a branch of the sea from here.

Our arrival there was, to say the least, unceremonious. It was in fact against the will of everyone concerned that we did arrive there at all, and yet when we did land, it filled our hearts with joy. What I have written is a little paradoxical I admit, but when I have related this ower true tale, the above statement will no longer seem a puzzle. Where to begin I hardly know unless I blurt it right out and say, "We were shipwrecked." Don't be alarmed, *'cos I ain't ded yit.*

The following is an account of the loss of the Schooner *Alice Dell* with the attendant circumstances showing how it was I came to be there, instead of *bein a whum i' bed.*

The 8th Regt. left Fortress Monroe on the 31st May '65, on board the splendid U.S. Mail Steamship *Illinois* with three Brigadier Generals aboard with their respective Staff Officers. After a charming voyage of ten days we arrived in Mobile Bay and landed for about twenty-four hours, a couple of miles above Fort Morgan. We had a good time there. I went to a ball with Colonel Armstrong, Major Pell and a few other officers and while there rather surprised them by my proficiency playing the piano.

We re-embarked about 10 o'clock, the 11th inst., and dropped anchor on the 15th outside the bar at the mouth of the Rio Grande and about 3 miles from Brazos Santiago, our destination, which is as near as such a vessel can safely get. There was a very heavy sea, and when the government boat steamed up to us, it was found to be an impossibility to get the troops on board. Both vessels rolled and tossed so much that their respective spars would sometimes make to each other an angle.

We waited a day, but the sea continued to be rough and as the supply of water began to diminish rapidly under the drinking powers of 1,200 men it was resolved to get the troops ashore if possible. A schooner, the Alice Dell, was towed alongside as near to the vessel as could be with safety and with the aid of row boats seven of the Companies, including the Co. A. to which I belong, were put aboard the schooner. We lay there waiting to see if the swell would diminish but as evening approached with no improvement, the pilot came aboard to take us in. The sails were hoisted with some difficulty owing to the crowded state of the decks. The breeze freshened and the sea became worse than ever. As we went along I noticed that at a distance of something like half a mile from the shore there was a white streak of foam, where the waves seemed to break with great fury. This was caused by a sand bar only about three or four feet from the surface of the water. Through this obstruction the pilot told me there was only two channels for the schooner to pass through and that he anticipated a little difficulty in making the passage. We were coming right to the breakers, when the pilot sung out. "Captain, lower away the peak of your foresail and stand by to hoist up the jibs."

"Aye aye, Sir."

"Hoist up your Jibs."

"Aye aye, Sir. Haul on dem ropes so queek as you can," sung out the captain, who was a Dutchman.

"Be lively Captain. Why the devil don't you hoist away?"

"Haul. Haul. Haul!! Gott verdamm. Oh de ropes are foul of de block. Vat can I do. I cannot do anyting. De ropes are all foul. So mooch men. So mooch sea."

"Oh for Jesus Christ's sake do something. Send a man up aloft to clear away the ropes, or we shall all go to hell. Gentlemen, I can not steer the boat and work her both," said the pilot to the officers standing near him.

I noticed that the sea was white with foam all around us, and was seaman enough to know that the vessel would soon strike and therefore held on to the lower rigging, like grim death to a dead nigger. All at once she struck with a force that sent nearly everyone sprawling. The wheel spun round and sent the pilot head over heels against the bulwarks.

The vessel spun round so as to bring her broadside to the wind and then the sea began to break over us. The next thing water began to come into the hold. The pumps were rigged and manned. Then we let go the anchor and set the mains'l and by that means worked the vessel round, so as to get her head to the wind. In that position she did not labor so heavily and there was every probability that she would hold together till the next morning.

The swell was so heavy that each roll she made caused her to drag the anchor a little and we were gradually getting nearer to the beach

141

but even this was alarming for just between us and the shore were the remains of a wreck of a steamer which occurred there a few years ago. The ironwork stands looming out of the water and the pilot said it would be better to go to pieces where we were than strike against the old wreck.

As everything possible had been done we went down into the cabin and the old Dutchman got us some tea and made us as comfortable as possible and begged us to make a favorable report to the government in order that he would get paid for his vessel. We told him there was no certainty that we would make any more reports in this world. He however seemed certain that we should get ashore in the morning.

Capt. Miller is a first rate swimmer, and did not seem at all anxious about his own safety so he said to the Chaplain,

"Can you swim, sir?"

"No."

"Trust in God then."

"There is many a worse trust you may make than that," answered the chaplain.

The night seemed a very long one and we were all glad to see the break of day. The Colonel was not aboard with us. He had gone ashore in a small boat from the Illinois and had seen our misfortune and signal of distress but had been unable to render or obtain any assistance. But at dawn of day he had a boat ready with some men and came to us and took about ten men ashore. By this time the tide was rising and and as the pumps had been going all night the vessel was afloat, and by paying out the cable we brought the vessel within a hundred fathoms of the beach. Then by means of the boat a rope was passed to the shore, and we were enabled to pass the men ashore pretty quickly. At 4 o'clock in the afternoon we were all ashore safe and sound.

Sharks are very plentiful but there was so many men in the water that the noise and splashing they made frightened them all away. We got across to this place by means of lighters. It is a flat, sandy island devoid of vegetation and no fresh water. If you dig down you obtain water but it is as salt as the sea. All the water we use except some carried from the Rio Grande is obtained by condensing sea water. This is about the worst thing about the place. Fish are plentiful and there is always a good supply of government stores.

142

There is also a breeze during the greater part of the day which is very pleasant. Mosquitos and sandflies and gnats generally abounding in this region are quite scarce in Brazos de Santiago. I think I have now given you the most interesting facts I can think of. I ought to say however that on the whole I like my position and am rapidly acquiring the tactics of infantry.

I have sent to the New York Post Office for any letters that may be there for me, but until further notice I wish you would address as on the fly leaf of this letter.

Give my love to Miss Mort, William Sutcliffe and John G. Haas. Also to Mr Knox and that is about all. Oh. No, not quite. My love to Coz. Rachel and Miss Isabella Hartley. Kind remembrances to Betty Knowles and Owd Maria, and to the Tongue family especially Lucy—"Miss Lucy had a baby, she dressd it all in white etc" Give my kindest remembrances to Mr Barlow and the bitterest kind of silent contempt to a family which shall be nameless.

Hoping you are all well at home, with the greatest affection I remain,

Your Jamie.

P.S. I post this the 25th June 1865. Write as soon as you receive it.

Master Peter H. Goo lad Pether!! Hooray!! Dit ger afore eawr Walther. Ay. Eh mon ah am fain. Theaw mun keep afore him if to con.

I don't know what to tell you besides what I have said in the other letters but I was very glad to read your letter and will answer the next one you write with a longer than this.

Your affectionate Bro. in haste
Andrew Ross

Camp 8th U.S. Col Troops. Infy.
2nd Brig. 2nd Div. 25th A.C.
near Rio Grande City, Tex.
July 28th 1865

My Dear Mother,
Since writing my last, I have taken a short walk with the Regiment from Brazos Santiago to Rio Grande City—150 miles. The second

day of the march was about the hardest. It was through a Chapporal or Jungle in the burning heat of a tropical sun. Eight men of our Regiment on that day's march dropped down and died. Thank goodness I had no knapsack or musket to carry, and I had taken the precaution to fill my canteen with claret wine and a little water, which just lasted me to the end of the march. (That day's march I mean.) The third day, we passed through Brownsville, a city of some importance. The country we passed through had a sameness that was quite wearisome. But there were many curious and interesting things to be seen—snakes of various kinds. We killed at least twelve rattlesnakes on the way. There are some millions of lizards, an abundance of mosquitoes and creeping things, tarantulas or poisonous spiders, *scorpions* and above all the horned frog of Texas, which has six or eight horns upon its head and a body and tail like a crocodile. The birds are of the gayest hues. I saw one today, a brilliant magenta colour. One bird at least sings sweetly. That is the mocking bird. I once heard a nightingale but I think the mocking bird goes a little ahead of him. The plants and flowers are all tropical, the cactus, mesquit, palmetto, swamp lilies, sun flowers etc, etc.

Since our arrival here, I have been appointed Regimental Quartermaster, so that I have now a horse to ride, and am a field officer. Captain Miller is very sorry that the Colonel has detailed me for Quartermaster. He says he never gets a good officer but someone takes him away.

The people we saw on the march and those living here in Rio Grande City are nearly all Mexican and neither speak or understand English. This part of the country was taken from Mexico in the war with that country less than twenty years ago. They seem to be a mixture of Indian and Spanish and the language they speak is also a mixture of the same, I understand. They seem to be a very ignorant and most uncivilized race. Imagine the lady of the house going to make dinner. She slaughters a goat or sheep to commence with. And after skinning the animal, cuts up the parts she does not want to use, in strips, and hangs them up like clothes upon a line to dry in the sun; then chops up the selected piece for dinner, and stews it in a pan over the fire—gipsy fashion. Then to make bread she has two rough stones, one flat and the other like a scythe stone only longer with which she rubs and bruises Indian corn until it has the consistency of

144

dough. And then she makes little balls of it and rolls each one into a cake about the size and thickness of crumpets. When these are baked and the stew is ready, with a bowl of milk the dinner is complete. These people do not seem to have an idea of the luxuries or even the comforts of civilized life.

July 29th 65. Last night after I had retired for the night the doctor called me out of my first slumber, to help him secure a huge tarantula that was making a tour of observation round the walls of his tent. It was the most horrible looking spider I ever saw. It could not be less than three inches from tip to tip and both legs and body were covered with hair. A bite from one of these things it is said will kill a horse. After some trouble we secured the brute and sent him to rusticate in the inside of a glass case filled with alcohol. The company he found there was not numerous but very select, consisting of two scorpions, one lizard of a venomous kind and an ant, an inch-and-a-half long. Just as we had seen the tarantula safely to his future home, a large beetle attracted by the light buzzed into the tent and after knocking against the doctor's head he bounced against the candle and knocked it over leaving us in total darkness. I ran out and made my way to my own tent, leaving the doctor in the lurch with the beetle, and I heard him for ten or fifteen minutes afterwards striking the sides of the tent with a towel or something in his convulsive efforts to get rid of the unwelcome intruder.

I can not tell you for what reason all these troops have been sent down here. I thought it was to be a war with Mexico, but no demonstrations in that way have been made as yet. The troops have been strung out along the Rio Grande as if the object was merely to guard the frontier and the only reason I can suggest is that the U.S. Govt. wishes to prevent the shipping of cotton without payment of export dues.

The only water we have to drink is Rio Grande which is so muddy that if a saucer is filled with it the bottom can not be seen, and if a tumbler be filled and allowed to stand for an hour or so, a deposit of mud is made at the bottom at least half-an-inch thick. But after it has settled it is pretty good water. Much better certainly than the condensed water we were compelled to use at Brazos Santiago.

There are only two Regiments here. General Jackson, the Commander of the Division, has his headquarters here and he always keeps our Regiment near him, as he considers the men of the 8th to be the most gentlemanly of any in the Corps.

Our Lieut. Colonel is a man of about 30 years of age and unmarried. He was wounded at the Battle of Olustee in Florida, and after nearly a year's absence he rejoined the Regiment at Fortress Monroe when on the way here. He is just about the best officer in the Regiment and certainly the greatest favorite in the Regiment, not even excepting the Colonel himself.

I have just enough employment as Regimental Quartermaster to prevent *ennui* and not so much as to make me weary. In fact I am very comfortably situated. I often wonder how you are getting along, whether the looms are working or not, and how you all are and how you all look. It was two years last May since I left home. There have been changes made since then—I mean in appearance. Sister Annie and Bros. Walter, Peter and Benjamin I suppose have changed most.

I am expecting a letter from you every time the mail comes up. I am getting quite anxious to hear from you, and beg you will write to me as soon as possible after receiving this.

I am enjoying good health, and hope you all have the same blessing. I do not think I have much more to add. I hope Miss Mort is well and as blooming as ever. Give my love to her.

After dress parade last evening the Colonel as usual had all the officers up to his tent, to talk things over and suggest improvements etc and after he had done with military subjects he concluded in the following words with which I will close my letter.

"Gentlemen, I think I have spoken of everything that I intended to speak of, and I have only one thing more to add and that is "Be Virtuous and Be Happy.""

Your Jamie

Rio Grande City, Texas
July 31st 1865

My Dear Bro. Joseph,

I have just this moment received and read your letter dated May 12th and 15th and directed to the battery. I had sealed up my letter and have been compelled to open it again in order to enclose this. I also enclose part of the envelope so as to give you an idea that it has travelled some.

It takes a month for a letter to come here from New York. I have read of the prosperity of the looms and the growing part of our family with great pleasure. I am glad you received my Carte de Visites. I had never heard from them and had begun to believe they had "mizzled". Especially I feel satisfied that Miss Mort was gratified. You are right about the Uniform. I was in my *fatigue* or *second best* uniform. The blouse or coat is dark blue and the stripes on the sleeve a brilliant scarlet. The buttons gilt. I had on however a pair of black trousers made by Alanson of Farnworth.

About the Confederate Notes, I am sorry that I cannot send you any more as the inhabitants hereabouts do not care for notes of any kind and never had any money, only Mexican and Spanish coins. When in Richmond I could have got any quantity of them. I had a thousand dollar coupon (Confederate) and would have sent it but it would have cost half a dollar postage, it was so heavy, and I gave it away.

I received the London *Punch* you mention and also a copy of the London *Times* for which I thank you. I am very sorry to hear of the death of Poor Tom Constantine. I agree with you in thinking that a certain bog-trotter of the Emerald Isle has put his foot in it by leaving his treacle business for the more uncertain one of cotton. He is a mean skunk. "Let him rip."

You do not mention Bro. William in your letter. I suppose his star is still rising and increasing Brilliancy.

With regard to curiosities. If only I had the means, I could make some valuable contributions to any museum. I never saw one of the horned frogs of Texas in any collection of curiosities, and think it is the most curious living thing that I ever did see. But I should want some spirit of wine to preserve it in or if I was coming myself I would bring a live one. I have the rattle off a rattlesnake's tail. I could get scorpions, lizards, snakes, tarantulas, camelions and many curious insects and birds if I only had the means of preserving and transporting them.

I think Martin Johnson & Co. have been genuine friends to the family and also Mr Wigglesworth in good wishes at least. You do not mention my mother once in your letter.

General Armstrong and *me* and a few more of the staff intend to go out hunting in a few days. There are plenty of deer about ten miles North of this, and rabbits in abundance quite near. One was shot this morning close to camp nearly as big as a Jackass. He had ears 6½ inches long. Fact, 'pon honor.

I got acquainted with a gentleman in Rio Grande City who has been in this part of the country many years and who speaks the language like a native who has promised to take me over to Comago, a city on the Mexican side about 5 miles from here, and introduce me to some rich señoritas.

I am studying Mexican like a brick, or at least I ought to say trying to pick it up. I can already give the morning and evening salutations, and ask for milk or water or for a light—and tell a señorita she is pretty—and ask, "What do you call that." Don't you think I am going ahead?

I am going to a "fandango" before long.

But the Mexicans are treacherous as devils and so jealous that if you look at a man's wife, your life is unsafe if he only gets a chance at you. The part of Mexico near here is in a state of Anarchy. Cortenas holds it but he and his men are only a gang of robbers.

Write soon—and let it be a long letter—and oblige

Your affectionate brother
James

Camp 8th Reg U.S. Col. Troops. Infy.
2nd Brig 2nd Div 25th A.C.
Ringgold Barracks, Texas
Via New Orleans   Aug 19th 1865
My Dear Bro. William,

I received your letter on the 17th inst. and read it with much interest, especially the account of the trip to "Houghton Tower". You say in your epistle that I seem to be stouter than I used to be. I believe I am, but I am sure I am a different Colour. I was once celebrated for a white face. I would bet a month's pay that if you saw me today you would say I had the darkest complexion of any of the family of Horrocks's that you are acquainted with. The sun of Virginia and the South has tanned me considerably. I have just been looking through the glass and find my neck is about the complexion of a Mexican—that is, copper colored. There is nothing of a woman about me. When I speak I make men jump.

Today I took the liberty of countermanding the orders of Bat. Brig. Genl. Armstrong. Consequence is that his orders have been disobeyed; mine have been obeyed. I expect of course that I shall have to explain myself for taking such a liberty, but if he is at all stiff about it, I know how to take him down a peg.

I wish you knew enough about the Regulations of the U.S. Army to understand exactly the position and power I have, and you would be more surprised than you are now that I have ever attained to the position of Regimental Quartermaster.

It is such a position that even my superiors in rank are very glad to be on good terms with me, because I have it in my power to do them many favors—*or not*—just as I like. Now for instance I will give you verbatim as near as possible a conversation which took place today.

Scene—My tent—Ross writing—Servant in attendance etc
Time 10 a.m.

CAPTAIN KRIBS   Quartermaster, I shall take it as a great favor if you will let me have the use of your wagon to make an arbor for my tent.

ROSS, R.Q.M.   You can't have it.

Exit Capt. Kribs.

Again—Scene, the same, a little later

MAJOR PELL   Quartermaster, how would a glass of nice cool claret go?

ROSS   (*indifferently*) Well Major, it would be better than a kick in the stomach by a stallion.

MAJOR P.   Well come this way a moment.

Scene—The Major's Tent—Ross drinking claret

MAJOR P.   Mr Ross, I have a favor to ask of you.

ROSS   Spit it out, Major.

MAJ. P.   I should like your man, Davis, to fix my bedstead.

ROSS   He shall do it sir, first thing tomorrow morning. He is otherwise employed at present. Pass the cigars, Major.

I have a nice wall tent, all to myself. I have one man for a cook, one man to look after my horse and one man for a valet de chambre.

149

I have not a cent in my pocket but my credit is unbounded and I want for nothing.

Aug 25th. I went over to Comargo day before yesterday. It is a large town (large for this country), about five miles in the interior of Mexico. It is held by General Cortenas, who is anti-Maximilian. I had an introduction to him and also to his brother, Colonel Cortenas.

Gen. Cortenas has the reputation of being a great robber, but his looks belie him if it is true. He is a stout gentleman who does not look as if he ever shed a drop of human blood in his life, and was very courteous to me, and told me to send him word when I was coming again and he would send a bodyguard to protect me from the rascals who infest the country between the river and the city of Comargo.

I enclose a ticket I got for a Grand Ball in Comargo. Unfortunately I could not stay as I had already stayed longer than I had any permission to.

I do not know Emma Yates unless it is the Emma who used to go to the Seminary when I was a youngster, with her Bro., John, who died.

Give my love to Everybody who has the same feeling for me, and believe me always the same affectionate Bro.
James

Ringgold Barracks, Texas
Aug 23rd 1865
My Dear Bro. Joseph,
To use the eulogistic and expressive words of a brother officer, "You are a Bully Boy with a glass eye," or to borrow an equally unique expression, "You are a double pressed, gilt edged 'brick'." What for? First, for writing me such a long and interesting letter. Secondly, for beating everybody at Draughts. Thirdly, for a woman's reason, *because you are.*

Talking about a woman necessarily brings one to the feminine gender. (Fact 'pon honor.) And on that subject permit me to say that you have made me interested in the highest degree in that charming Miss Mary—"only Nineteen years old". Of course you know I mean Uncle Adam's Daughter. It is so very seldom you speak of a girl at all that I am bound to believe that this *dear little Mary* must be possessed of a superlative, refined, and doubly distilled essence of all the sweetest and most loveable qualities of the daughters of Eve (and she has reason to be proud when the fame of her loveliness has penetrated into the wilds of Texas).

At the present moment I have a bottle of French Absinthe and half-a-dozen bottles of Claret in my tent, and I am willing to give the whole lot for a look at "fair Mary" ye virgin weaver of ye city of Bolton. . . . However the fates forbid me such a treat and, as *Mr Toots* would say (while his heart was bleeding inwardly), "It is of *no consequence at all, not the slightest.*"

I am delighted to hear of my mother's good health and the prosperity and comfort of the whole family. I received Bro. William's Letter and have partly written an answer to it a few days ago which I will enclose with this. His letter seems to have been posted with yours or at least about the same time, and I know of no reason why they should not have come together as the direction is *prezackly* the same on each.

I also received the *Wigan Examiner* and the *Manchester Examiner and Times* with your letter last night for which I thank you, but did not get the Preston paper you speak of as containing the history of the Horrocks family. And while on the subject I must apologise for not sending you any American papers lately. I will only give one of my seventeen reasons. I have not had any to send. In fact I have not seen a Newspaper worth anything since I left Mobile. The American News contained in the Papers you sent me were actually news to me.

I have heard some nice pieces lately and have learned to sing them. If you are still a lover of music—I am sure you are—buy them. They are:

1. Her Bright Smiles Haunt Me Still
2. Beautiful Dreamer by Stephen C. Foster
3. Then You'll Remember Me
4. Love's Chidings

I am in the tail end of the universe. Most of the people round here are half-savage. There are of course exceptions. There are no vegetables raised in this part of Texas, and if we had not a very liberal government I do not know what would become of all the

Troops down in this outlandish place. The houses are either the rudest kind of log huts, or are built of bricks of dried mud. Children run round naked, and the women do not have by any means an extravagant amount of dress on. Of course they have generally rather a gay dress for a Fandango, and that is about the only occasion they seem to care for it.

There is no church on this side of the river but some of them I believe attend a Roman Catholic place of worship on the Mexican side in a town called Comago.

Captain Brooks (a nice young person for a small party, by the way) says that if the world was a bull this would be the "ass hole".

Another officer headed a letter home thus:

Camp Distress
Fifteen miles from the knowledge of God,
Date unknown

You speak of my leaving the army and entering a mercantile house in New York or some other large city. At the present time I would not go to New York if I left the army, nor to any city North. There have been so many thousands of soldiers discharged that the markets are overcrowded at present with every kind of capacity, and if I was there, there are ten chances to one whether I should get a situation worth while or not. I know I can get my own living but that ain't the thing. I want to make money *fast*, and if I was discharged from the service here, should probably go to the gold region of Senora in Mexico, or else take the steamer at Brazos Santiago for California. But I am going to stay in the service about long enough to have $500 clear on leaving it after paying all my debts. At the present moment my credits and debits show a balance of only $200 in my favor. You must remember I have had to buy a great many articles of dress at a ruinous price: $15.00 for a pair of boots, $5.00 for a hat uniform, three dollars for a straw hat and everything else in Ratio.

I went down to Edinburgh about a fortnight ago (fifty miles from here) in charge of a train of wagons, with guards etc. The country is almost uninhabited and abounds in game. I saw one flock of wild turkeys but could not get near enough to kill any of them. They run so fast just like ostriches. And Oh! the flocks of pigeons, turtle doves, quails, prairie hens and lots of deer and rabbits—and squirrels.

I also saw several wolves and any quantity of snakes.

But altho' I had a great deal of pleasure on the excursion I also had my share of trouble. The river was very high and in consequence there was many places where the road was submerged in water. In one place there was a mile of it at one stretch covered with water and in each case I had to ride through it myself first before I could risk taking the wagons through. The place I have mentioned was very deep in the middle for about 20 yards. It took my horse just over the back and I had to cross this style . . . I knew of course that the mules (there were six to each wagon) would have to *swim* and as the wagons were empty I knew they would float, so I placed two men in each wagon with orders that if the mules swerved off the proper course or got entangled in the traces, as they are very apt to do in such a case, to jump into the water and take hold of them and assist to get them through. I had more then half the men in the water before I got the wagons safely over, and we had on the whole a pretty tough time, but by dint of perseverance and good management we all got safely across. And on the return journey with full wagons the water had subsided about four feet and we had no difficulty.

I will conclude with love to my Mother in Bushels—and *pecks* of love to my brothers and sister and Miss Mort, and also you may tell Miss Mary Horrocks that she has the kindest regards of a Lieutenant in the U.S. Army,

James Horrocks

Camp 8th U.S.C.I.
near Brownsville, Texas
Novr 1st 1865

My Dear Bro. Joseph,

The 8th U.S.C.I. is being mustered out of the service by reason of orders from the War Dept. and we are now on the way home. I am mustered out to remain in the Department as I think New Orleans is a very likely place for me to get along. On the 29th Octr I was relieved from duty as Acting Regimental Quartermaster and turned over the property to O. W. Norton, the R.Q.M. of the Regiment. It has been quite a job. I had about $20,000 dollars worth of Govt.

property on my hands including Horses, mules, harness equipments, Wagon, Clothing, tools, Tents etc, etc for every item of which I was responsible in the strictest sense of the word—but I have transferred the whole of it and sent in my final returns, rendering a straight account of my stewardship.

As I told you before I stay in New Orleans. My muster out is dated 10th Nov '65. By that time I expect to be in New Orleans, a citizen once more after a military career of more than two years.

I do not regret my military experience by any means but I am glad to get out of the service for one reason if not for another.

I have no acquaintance in New Orleans and shall of course resume my patronymic. The Regiment goes north and the probabilities are that I shall see none of them any more.

I shall try and get employment in some Cotton Merchants—and will take a situation at a low salary if I can get it in an establishment. To my mind, who knows but in a short time my employers may send me on to Liverpool on business—Wouldn't that be fun? Eh!

We have had considerable rain since we came here.

A few nights before we left Ringgold Barracks, the Officers stationed there, in number about 50, gave a grand ball to the Ladies of Rio Grande City and Comargo. It was a grand affair. The refreshments and lights alone cost 500 dollars. We had 50 young Señoritas from the two cities. I danced every set, and every dance. I took the belle of the evening twice for a partner. Oh the little ducks. A little girl about 10 years of age was about the best dancer in the room, and she spoke English. She danced with me the oftenest. I afterwards learned that she had the most *oro* of any girl in that room.

We had chandeliers of glittering bayonets, festoons of evergreens, transparencies and all such. We also had a magnificent band of string music. Oh, the wine that was drunk and Oh, the fun I had that night. I had learned about a dozen Spanish polite sentences, such as, "Will you do me the favor to dance with me, Señorita,"; "Let us promenade Miss,"; "Would you like some refreshment?"; "Many thanks."

I know I looked well that night having a good suit of uniform on, and felt just in good trim for enjoying it.

That night is something to look back on with pleasure. I shall never forget it.

Brazos Santiago, Texas, Nov 6th. Since writing the above I have come down to Brazos and have received a letter from Bro. Henry giving me a very interesting account of an important ceremony.

I had half completed a letter to him when I left Ringgold Barracks but must write another which I will do, and enclose it in this. Reading it you will find that I have slightly altered my plans for the future.

Au Revoir
your Bro. James

> Camp 8th U.S.C.I.
> Brazos Santiago, Tex.
> Nov 6th 1865

My Dear Bro. Henry,

I give you joy. I Congratulate you on your happy and I think well chosen change of life. My new Sister Betsy, I wish you every happiness, a long life free from connubial quarrels, and a nice little pile of pledges of affection etc, etc.

By Jove, Harry my boy, Mrs H. H. looks lovely in both pictures you sent me, and so does my dear Mother, God bless 'em both.

I should like to pop in and see you one of these days but circumstances at present will not admit of it. Now I must speak of myself.

In the old Battery there was a young fellow I thought a great deal of. We bunked together for a long while and I once sent you a picture of his sister, Miss C. M. Vallade. His name is George E. Vallade.

He has a business turn and wrote to me in Texas after the Battery was mustered out, saying he had about $6,000, and would like to come to Texas to go into business. I immediately made arrangements with the officers in power to have him sutler for the Regt. and wrote on for him to come down and take the position. At Brazos I got a letter from him stating that he had started for Texas on receipt of my letter but when he arrived in New Orleans learned that the Regiment was to be mustered out immediately. Under these circumstances he had looked around him and made up his mind to go into business at Indianola, Texas, and he writes to me saying that he can make a good thing of it if he has only some one to help him and he begs and prays me to come on to Indianola and go into partnership with him after I have squared accounts with the U.S.A. paymaster.

I have written to him to tell him I will come, and you must direct your next letters to Mr James Horrocks:

Care of George E. Vallade Esq.
Indianola, Texas,
U.S. of America.

I received a copy of *fun* from you yesterday for which I thank you.

Along with this letter I shall post a newspaper, containing a little present to my dear sister-in-law. It is a gold dollar with a ribbon in it, which I obtained under the following circumstances. The day before I left Ringgold Barracks I went up to a christening at Judge Stewarts. It was a Roman Catholic ceremony, and the godfather and godmother were Mr & Mrs Clay Davis who own the whole of Rio Grande City.

After the ceremony the godfather and godmother presented a souvenir to each person present. This is a Mexican custom I believe. Mr Davis gave me a dime, about the size of a sixpence and Mrs Davis pinned this identical gold dollar on my coat. I think a great deal of it and therefore give it to your handsome wife. I hope she will get it safe.

I think if I once get started I shall make money in this country.

You must excuse me if I make this letter short. I am rather pressed for time and expect to start for New Orleans tomorrow or the day after. I hope you will continue to do well at the mill. I have not done very well so far but I might have done worse.

After I have paid my debt and bought a new suit of clothes I expect to have from 300 to 400 dollars clear, with which of course I shall go in with Vallade. I may sink the whole of it but I rather think I shall increase it. I shall try devilish hard to make it three or four thousand and then thirty or forty thousand and then I'll come home and leave someone to carry on my share of the business.

I will now conclude, hoping you will excuse this illegible scrawl. Try for my sake to make it out. And believe me to remain with undying love for you all

Your affectionate brother
James

My Dear Bro. Peter,

I thank you for your letter and just write this in order to encourage you to write to me again. I am very much horrified to learn that Bro. William has taken a skeleton into his house, and especially such a one as that of the horrid old Betty Eccles.

Your sage remark concerning little Irish Henry Duffy displays a wisdom above your years. Anyone who leaves the certainty of a competence for the probability or chance of riches is nothing less than a tup head.

I think you must be a very good singer from what you say in your letter, as no one is better able to judge than your mother. She might well be frightened when you went up the chimney pipe with Steeple Jack. If you had by chance fell from the summit I should not have the pleasure of hearing you *warble* as I intend to have when I come home. You say you are growing rapidly. How high are you now?

New Orleans is quite a large city. In appearance it does not look very much unlike Liverpool but the river steamboats give the port itself rather a different appearance. American steamboats are different in style altogether to English boats, but you have probably seen pictures of them. They are much lighter and far more elegant both inside and out than ours.

Peter, it is going on for three years since I saw you. I suppose that you and Walter and Benjamin have altered so much during that time that I shall hardly know you.

You are now nearly 14 years of age and I suppose, by the time I come home you will be wearing a stove pipe hat and a coat with long tails, and will probably be able to play better on the piano than I can.

I was trying to play yesterday and found that my fingers had forgotten their former skill and I was very much disappointed with myself. You tell me that the Laughing Chorus and a few others you have learnt are better than the ones I mention. If that is so, they must be very pretty indeed. But I do not think you have heard the ones I mentioned.

But Good Bye, Pee, I must conclude. With love,

Your James

New Orleans
26th Nov 1865

My Dear Bro. Benjamin,

I read your very nice letter with much pleasure. I was in the camp of my Regiment at the time. There was scarcely any officers there besides myself but you would stare if you could see the soldiers. There is about one thousand of them and they are all black and they have such white teeth and big rolling eyes, and if I was walking along and met one of them you would see him bring his heels together, stand still and touch his hat as I passed. That is because I am an officer and they all know that if they did not show that respect for me I would have them tied up to a tree for a little while in order to teach them manners.

I was very sorry to hear of Mrs Tong's death, which I think Bro. Henry mentioned in his letter nearly a month ago. But it is sad all the same. Henry might have been lying to me, but as you say she died, I know it must be so and will buy some crape by and by.

It was very sad that the carrier of Samuel Hays should come to such a full stop. I did not know him but I am sorry that could not find his nose, because he might have been fond of snuff, and now alas! he has got nothing to sneeze with.

Be a good lad Bendigo. Work hard at your books and you will become a man, if you have good luck, at least a week before your maternal guardian. Practice walking on your head as much as possible, as you may have to emigrate to New Zealand where the people, I am told, walk with their feet uppards. And if you become proficient you will be able to beat them at their own game, which will give great joy to all your relatives.

I understand you are going to school yet. Now Ben, pay attention. If your teacher gives you any sauce, you sauce back. And if he continues to use abusive words it will show great courage on your part if you walk up to him and kick his shins. This will render you notorious, and if you succeed in inspiring him with a wholesome dread of your brogans, it will be one great point gained. Also observe the same line of conduct with regard to your fellow pupils. If any of them hurt you, whether on purpose or not, you look at him all over, commencing at his cap and down to his feet and back again. Then if you think you can lick him, why lick him by all means, and then you may afterwards let him apologise. But if you cannot lick

158

him, it is a good way to go a little distance from him and then throw a stone at him and take to your heels. If he runs after you and you find he is gaining upon you, let him come pretty near to you and then turn round quickly and trip him with your head in the stomach. If you do this with sufficient force you are almost certain to knock the breath out of him. It will add to the effect if you ask him what he means by running against you in that vulgar manner. Do all these things and when I come home I will spank you. Write another letter to your dear brother,

James Horrocks

New Orleans (St Chas. Hotel)
Nov 27th 1865

My Dear Bro. Joseph,

I read your letter with great pleasure. Bro. William's "Carte" is very good indeed and I thank him for sending it. I enclose another of mine. I just had it taken for the purpose of showing you the uniform more than anything else.

All the officers of the Regiment begged me to let them have my picture. I tell you there is a great deal of pleasure in finding that you have gained the esteem and friendship of those who have been your constant companions for as long a time as the officers of the Regiment have been mine. Living as we did so as to see every side of each other's character, I felt quite gratified to find how well they all seemed to like me and crowded round me to say goodbye, pressing me to write to them and to let them have my autograph and address etc, etc.

I am the only officer left behind. All the rest are going North to be mustered out at Philadelphia with the Regiment. They left yesterday morning in the *Evening Star*. In all probability I shall see very few of them again. But I shall never forget them. They are such genial, good natured, gentlemanly fellows.

I have settled up my accounts with the government, and have been paid off.

I have paid all my debts, bought a new trunk of a splendid style and finish (sole leather), an excellent suit of citizen's clothes and everything I stood in need of and have still above $400 left. I am now waiting for a letter from Vallade at Indianola, to let me know what to invest my money in. If I do not hear from him before the 30th I shall go on to Indianola without investing any of it, and if I find only a poor prospect of doing well there I shall go on to Brazos Santiago, in the absence of any other engagement, where the Chief Quartermaster has promised to give me a Clerkship at $125.00 a month and a ration any time I will send him word and also to give me transportation at the expense of the Govt. to that place.

The passage to Indianola is about four days. I shall get there probably about the 4th of December.

You need not be afraid to direct your letters to me there as I will make arrangements in case I do not stay there, to have my letters forwarded to me.

Of course you will direct as I said in my last letter:
James Horrocks,
Care of George E. Vallade Esq.,
Indianola,
Tex.

It is rather surprising to find myself walking out at this time of the year in light garments and slippers and cotton socks, without taking cold. It is a gay climate to pass the winter in.

I am recommended also to the Secretary of War for a Lieutenancy in the 2nd U.S. Cavalry, which I shall no doubt have the opportunity of accepting or declining in a couple of months from now.

I have called at several Cotton Brokers in this city to ask for employment. I was met with cold refusals, at which I laughed in my sleeve. The independent fools did not know that they could not obtain my services at any ordinary price. I suppose they thought I was a poor needy devil, hard up for something at which to get my living and the fact of the matter was that I would not take a situation under any of them for $1,500 a year.

I could not help thinking how miserable I should feel if I had been destitute and depending on their kind considerations, for anything. I only called for fun because I had nothing else to do.

I believe New Orleans is full of business at present. It is very dear living here. All the Hotels charge the same rates, namely $4.00 a day for bed and board, and no less no matter how long you stay.

I headed this letter St Chas. Hotel but am now staying at a boarding house at $12 a week.

I went on board one of the Mississippi Steam boats this morning. I never saw a more magnificent boat in my life. The arrangements for the comfort and pleasure of the passengers surpasses everything of the kind I ever saw.

Nov 28th 1865. I made enquiries this morning about the fare to Indianola and find it to be $40.00 which is a most exorbitant price. I could go away up to Illinois for the same money. However it is unavoidable and I must pay it.

I received several papers from you which I read with much pleasure. I have sent you a few lately which I hope you will receive all right.

My health is excellent and I am impatient to commence to do business and make money. I start from New Orleans the day after tomorrow on the *Reindeer.*

Remember me to Mr Barlow, Mr S—, to Wm. Sutcliffe and all who are in your opinion my well wishers.

Give my love to all the family of course including Mrs H. H.

I will write to Bro. William anon.

Your affectionate brother
James Horrocks

Epilogue

JAMIE DISEMBARKED AT Indianola, a thriving port in Calhoun County eleven miles southeast of present day Port Lavaca, on 5th December. George Vallade was nowhere to be seen. James therefore found himself some temporary work as clerk to the quartermaster of the military depot and on discovering, after a week, that Vallade was forty-five miles upcountry doing business he managed to arrange for himself to be sent there on official duties.

He set out in charge of a wagon-train with about a hundred horses and mules on a journey that lasted two days. He spent a couple of days at Victoria with Vallade, who promised to look out for an opening for him and warned him to be ready to be sent for soon.

Christmas Eve that year James spent at Chocolate Creek on his return journey, ten miles short of Indianola. He reached there in the dark in a buggy in the company of a new friend from Victoria. He stayed the night at the home of the bridge-keeper, a Mr Norris, who was also the owner of a large farm.

Mr Norris, unlike many in that part of Texas, was a former confederate who was quite happy to admit he had been a rebel and a good one at that. It did not take James long to become enchanted by Mr Norris's younger daughter. When he expressed an admiration for her sketches he was invited to visit the house again as her drawing teacher and began to wonder seriously how many cows and how much land it might be worth if he were to ask for her hand.

In the spring his plans were altered drastically. George Vallade and James had intended to open a store at Columbus, 150 miles in the interior. Vallade was to have run the store while Jamie acted as his agent on the coast, buying goods wholesale and shipping them upcountry to Columbus. However, about March, when James was going to set out for Columbus to join Vallade, he received an offer from a local tax inspector of a job as a clerk with a salary of $100 a month and the promise of becoming a deputy collector of taxes. At

163

this point he cut his links with Vallade and, in the company of the tax inspector, Mr Kingsbury, made his way back to Brazos Santiago and Brownsville in the southernmost tip of Texas.

It was not one of the safest of occupations. Nor, as he made clear to his brother Joseph, was the border a law abiding land in which to live:

> Murders in this country are of very frequent occurrence. It is not safe for a man to be on the street alone after dark. I met a friend of mine, a German whom I was acquainted with a Ringgold Barracks last summer. He told me that he and three officers, all acquaintances of mine, went over to Matamoros last week and were on the way to the Theatre when they were met and attacked by two men. Lieut. De Witt was shot dead and the rascals got away.

He suffered few regrets at having left the army:

> I accidentally met one of the men who belonged to the 5th N.J. Battery this morning. He was a Sergeant and is now a Corporal in the Light Artillery of the Regulars. He tells me that he was unable to get anything to do after the Battery was mustered out and lived there until his money was gone and then enlisted once more. When I saw him I felt a twinge of pity for myself to think that I was once clad in the same garb and subject to the same Regulations and laws. I think there is nothing could induce me to become a soldier again.
>
> I have seen a few different phases of life in my short career and of all the experience I have had that of a soldier seems to me the most miserable. As an officer of course it is quite bearable and in many respects very pleasant. But an enlisted man. Ugh! No more of it for *this* child.

Brownsville had its lighter moments. In June, for example, he watched a tightrope-walker cross the Rio Grande from Texas to Mexico. Then, as winter drew on, he enjoyed a busy social life, coming home from parties at three or four o'clock in the morning.

Sometimes he thought of returning home but the opportunities that England could give him seemed minimal compared with what America had to offer. Also there was the problem of Martha J.

Hamer to be considered. In November he broached the matter with Joseph:

> The entire cost of the Hamer claim to date would probably be now 3 years and ½ at ½ crown a week—£23. Charges of the court about £3-£26.
> I wish you would find out how much they will take to clear the bill and if not too much I will send them a draft for the amount. Considering the uncertainty of my ever returning, I should think she would be glad to take £30 and give me absolution for all the dues past, present and prospective. If she won't, she may go to h—.

That winter James's work was transferred to Galveston. In the spring he was sent out from Galveston to Millican, at the end of one of the railroads, and from there, in a horse drawn buggy, it was his responsibility to go out and collect the government's taxes. In many respects he was lucky to be a veteran of the Union army. It did help him find work, even if his present occupation had its disadvantages. He confided in Joseph, on his return from a two month tour around nine counties in the northern part of the district, "The people amongst whom I have been living are noted for their ruffianism and hatred to the Yankees." Nonetheless it was quite pleasant to find himself being addressed as Captain. "I am very much respected if not feared. The peaceful and good citizens are generally very anxious to have my friendship, and the roughs and rowdies would like to lodge a couple of slugs into me."

All the while, he was keeping an open eye for business opportunities and occasionally his thoughts turned once again to shipping cotton to Farnworth. On a different occasion he certainly did miss an opportunity:

> Petroleum has been discovered about sixteen miles east of Nacogdoches. If I was a Capitalist I would buy some land up in that country. The people are poor from the effects of the war and want to sell some of their lands.

One thing he did not foresee himself becoming was a teacher: "What a stupid life it seems to me now—that of teaching school. I am glad I did not settle down to such a tame occupation." Yet the autumn was to show that, if James had remained a schoolteacher in

England, he might have been in less danger of losing his life.

From Edgworth that October William sent Joseph a notice that had appeared in *The Lancet*: "Sad accounts come to hand of the prevalence of yellow fever in Texas." In Galveston only three out of twenty-six customs officers were reported fit for duty. The remainder were dead or ill. So slowly did news travel from Texas that by the time the family at home heard about the epidemic, the worst was already over.

Like many others in Galveston, Jamie Horrocks had fallen victim to yellow fever. He was lucky in having someone to take care of him—a lady who, when James first settled in Galveston, had told him she would nurse him if ever he caught the fever. She was a plump, cheerful married woman in her early thirties called Jennie Caldwell.

Jennie took James into her own house and for four days and four nights she did not leave his side for more than an hour, even then arranging for a friend of hers to sit beside him. At times he became delirious and had to be held down but on the twelfth day he was well enough to sit up and could write to his mother, "My hand is unsteady and I am otherwise a nervous and rather used up child." As a thank you when he recovered he gave Jennie a gold ring set with a pearl and, rather ominously, sent her love and her photograph to his mother.

By the end of October he was out on his rounds once more, risking life and limb amongst the unwilling taxpayers. In Piedmont he was lucky to find himself among Union supporters. Elsewhere in Texas he felt, "They would have no compunction at all in taking the life of any Yankee especially that of a Tax collector."

In July 1868, he gave a description of his daily routine at Galveston. He would rise at daybreak and work at the office for six hours without a rest. Then he would leave the office for the day and, in the evening, drive down to the beach and enjoy the sea breeze. At 9 p.m. he would retire to bed. He did not envisage spending the rest of his days in Galveston however. Texas was crippled by a post-war depression that was deteriorating from bad to worse. All the time James was building up his savings, trying to accumulate $2,000 in gold, after which he planned to move on to another state. In the late summer of 1868 he achieved his goal.

Setting out up the Mississippi, James travelled across country to

New York. There in September he took a passage on the steamship *Alaska* to Panama, crossed the isthmus by train and, aboard the steamship *Colorado*, on 3rd October 1868, sailed into San Francisco.

For two or three weeks James explored the region to the north of San Francisco, around Santa Rosa, looking for a place to make his home. At the end of the month he found it, Napa City, "one of the most delightful little cities in the world".

He had stopped smoking and put on weight and, in a letter to his brother Peter, maybe we can glimpse a little bit of his father. Peter, who seemed to share a kindred spirit, would have liked to have joined his brother in America. James felt unhappy when he learnt that Peter was employed at the mill, looking after the engine. There was more to life. He told him, "I have often wished that I understood how to use tools of various kinds and how to cultivate land and a great many other things I am entirely ignorant of. There are a thousand things that ought to be learned besides mere book learning."

At home Jamie's mother and brothers read with concern how Jennie Caldwell, now a widow, had come out to San Francisco in November to visit a relative. A warning letter from Joseph arrived too late. By the time James could read it, he and Jennie were already married. Not that the letter was likely to have made any difference. He threw it on the fire.

Jennie had some money of her own and, between the two of them, they rented a building beside the bridge at Napa City and named it the Collegiate Institute. In spite of his thoughts back in 1867, James had become the proprietor of a boys' school.

Their first few days at Napa City may have seemed to the couple like an idyll. They kept a cow, which became Jennie's pet, plenty of hens and chickens and a pig. They also had a garden and an orchard. Jennie did her own housework. She looked after the cow and the chickens, she washed, she scrubbed, she cooked and she baked. James's one regret was that she could not brew ale since they were both fond of it.

Among the fruit in the garden, he claimed there were two or three different varieties of grape, nectarines and apricots, half-a-dozen varieties of apple and different kinds of peach, plums, tomatoes, pears, cucumbers, pumpkins, green corn and watermelon. It was not worth the effort of trying to sell the produce because everywhere it was so cheap and plentiful.

In the flower garden, which took a bit of effort to look after, James discovered flowers which in England would never be seen outside a hothouse. Writing home he asked for some of the more familiar seeds, of buttercups, dandelions and daisies.

He also asked for some of his old books: Ovid's *Metamorphosis*, Greenwich's *Greek Grammar*, Xenophon's *Memorabilia*, a Greek lexicon, Maxwell's *English Grammar* and Colenzo's *Algebra*.

They also had a little lodger in their house, Robbie Woodward, the ten-year-old son of a wealthy rancher, sent to them for his education.

The work was hard. James found he had little time to himself. In addition to the usual lessons, several of the boys were studying Latin and one of them was learning Greek. It was as much as James could do in some cases to keep ahead of the pupils he was responsible for teaching.

In 1870 Jennie suffered a miscarriage and became ill.

Matters came to a head when the owner of the building in Napa City which the couple used as their home and school decided to sell it. The couple could not afford to buy. They had to find fresh premises or move out of Napa City. Making up their minds to leave, they set off northwards along the coast.

From Seattle they journeyed by steamer to Olympia at the head of Puget Sound. From there they hired a wagon to travel overland to Cowlitz landing. A canoe, oared by two half-breeds, brought them to Monticello at the confluence of the Cowlitz and the Columbia rivers. From Monticello they sailed by steamboat up the Columbia as far as Portland, Oregon, and then, buying a wagon and two mares, travelled 125 miles up the Williamette valley to Eugene City. The land they were going to they believed was fertile and agricultural and they were accompanied by an Edward A. Brown and his wife who planned to form a partnership with the Horrockses and breed sheep and cattle.

Unfortunately the business venture was not a success and, when Edward Brown's wife fell sick, he accompanied her back to Napa City.

The Horrockses stayed in Eugene City but by October James was teaching once again. "I am teaching music. Just think of it. What an idea. An acquirement obtained as a pastime is my means of livelihood. I am the only music teacher for twenty miles around." He had also taken work as chief clerk in the surveyor-general's office but it was only a temporary job.

The house where they lived was elegant enough and James liked burning wood on the fire. He still had no intention of returning to England. "Sometime I expect to come," he wrote, "if only for a visit but I do not think I could settle down to a plodding way of life such as I should have were I to return now."

However, Jennie was not getting better. She found the rainfall in Oregon depressing. A second Oregon winter, she told her husband, would kill her. In September 1871, James was sitting in the Cosmopolitan Hotel at Portland. Once again they were on the move but, this time, back eastwards.

They were making for St Louis, Missouri, a city that was prosperous and growing. In those days it was the fourth most populous city of the United States—after New York, Brooklyn and Philadelphia. Jamie saw it as a place of opportunity. One thing was certain: "I intend to stick permanently in St Louis this time."

For weeks he roamed St Louis looking for a job. Eventually, thanks to a letter of introduction from a friend in Eugene City, he found employment with the Mercantile Agency, a credit data company whose manager, Mr King, was a fellow Englishman. So comprehensive was the information stored there that James found a reference to his uncle Henry's business in Augusta, Illinois. In 1860 Henry was listed as a miller; in 1861, a hotel keeper; in 1868 in the brewery business with credit not good; and in 1869, no longer creditworthy.

True to his intention, James remained in St Louis. Unable to have any children of their own, he and his wife adopted a little girl. He stayed with the Mercantile Agency. It is just as well he had not made his home at Indianola. Hurricanes in 1875 and 1886 destroyed the town with the result that one of the busiest ports in Texas was removed from the map. A similar fate struck the port of Brazos Santiago.

Back in Lancashire, life for the Horrocks family had changed a great deal since January 1865. One Sunday, towards the end of that month, Jamie's father went to Bolton to visit a sick brother. On the way home that evening, he was coming down the steps to the platform at Bolton railway station when he dropped his ticket. Stooping to pick it up he overbalanced and fell head first on to the platform. His head received severe injuries. After a week and more of suffering, he died.

Ann, his widow, found herself the proprietress of a mill that was heavily mortgaged and with the debts of the business upon her shoulders. Joseph, assuming his responsibilities as head of the household, gave up his job with the Lancashire & Yorkshire Railway at Wigan, where he had become goods manager, to return home and try to get his father's business out of debt. Harry was at the mill too. Their first task was to try to raise a further loan in order to continue in business.

A spark of cheer was given to the whole family in August that year when Harry married his girlfriend of several years' standing, Betsy Mort, at the Farnworth Wesleyan chapel. All the Horrockses turned out to take part.

In spite of a brave effort, the attempt to save Mount Pleasant Mill was a failure and in the autumn of 1869 it had to be sold. The mother and younger children of the family lived on in Queen Street but Joseph applied for his old job again with the railway and became goods manager once more at Over Darwen.

Remaining unmarried, he took his work seriously and in a way that brought him into conflict with senior management. He was convinced that goods traffic on the railway could be handled with more efficiency and, in his attempt to promote the argument, he wrote a book. Although he received kind letters from publishers appreciating his work, they suggested it was aimed at too limited a readership to be a successful commercial venture. His book eventually appeared in 1909 under the title, *Railway Rates—The method of calculating equitable rates and charges for merchandise carried on railways*. It was published privately by his nieces, Annie's daughters who, as his executrices, were carrying out one of his last requests.

Harry stayed in the hard pressed cotton trade. In the early 1870s we find him and Betsy with their little family in the Manchester area, first at Victoria Mill, Droylsden, and then with him as manager of the New Islington Mill in Ancoats.

In those days a number of Britons were being enticed abroad to help set up cotton mills in the Russian empire. Harry and his family, joining the migration, went to Finland where he became a manager of

170

the new Finlayson's cotton factory at Tampere. When he died, his brother Walter went to take his place there.

William, having completed his three year course of studies at Guy's Medical School, became a successful general practitioner in Edgworth and Turton. His work and the distance from Farnworth obliged him, in the spring of 1864, to give up his position as assistant secretary and librarian of Holland's Sunday school. In 1866 he was courting Miss Edna Tootel and, as a product of their marriage, she bore him three daughters. His work as a doctor spanned the range from pulling teeth to midwifery and surgery. On making his rounds, he would visit distant parts on horseback and kept a horse-drawn sleigh for some of the journeys across the moors.

The inland sea that James referred to in his letter to William of 19 April 1865 was a reservoir being created down in the valley. The dam was built just a little upstream from Turton Bottoms where the main road linked Turton with Edgworth. Its water was to serve the growing town of Bolton. Among the buildings that were drowned was William's childhood home at Nicodean. A few decades ago, in times of drought, it used to be possible to catch a glimpse of the ruins. Today, with further developments, the waters of this Wayoh reservoir are deeper than ever. Below Turton Bottoms even the Jumbles has been turned into a reservoir.

George, the fifth of the brothers and the one who came after Jamie, was possibly the least fortunate member of the brood. He was already a seaman by the time James left for America. He planned to visit Jamie there. From Calcutta in December 1863, he wrote home, "You did not give me James's address." Again, two months later, ". . . give me Bro. James's directions." In 1870 he specifically asked for James's present address because he was sailing to New Orleans and hoped to see him.

When he married the mother of his infant son in Liverpool in 1873, he begged his mother to write to her while he was away. Travelling the world, it was fairly likely that he would come down with a tropical disease. It was while he was on the steamship *Yoruba* and his legs had become swollen that on the morning of 14th May 1873, he hauled himself without warning up onto the ship's rail and simply tumbled over the side.

Annie was James's only sister. She stayed at Edgworth to help William after James went to America but moved back to Farnworth to help Joseph and Henry when William got married. James was living in Oregon when he learnt she was being courted by John Thomas Knowles, a member of a family that sold shoes in Over Darwen. She married John Knowles. They settled in Over Darwen and in later years she and her family shared their home with her brother Joseph. When Walter returned from Finland he settled beside them in Richmond Terrace.

Ben, the youngest of the brothers, followed Jamie's example in 1875 by going to Westminster College in London. He did become a teacher, in Over Darwen, or Darwen as it became known, as headmaster of one of Darwen's Wesleyan day schools. Like Joseph, he too came into conflict with higher authority and, after an argument over salary, he left the profession to work in the insurance of cotton mills.

The greatest mark of any of the brothers was made by Peter. From Mr Knox's school he went to Farnworth Grammar School. He then attended a course in classics at Manchester's Owen's College. (Joseph lent him a copy of *Euclid* to help.) In 1873, at the age of twenty and having already spent some time as a door-to-door collector of fees for his brother William, he followed William's example and began to attend a course of studies at Guy's Medical School in London. He qualified as a doctor and in 1903 became the chief obstetric physician at Guy's Hospital.

He shared James's spirit of adventure. His love of mountaineering brought him to the attention in 1894 of the *Daily Graphic*. He was climbing the Zinalrothorn mountain in Switzerland. The guide on one side of him slipped and fell, jerking Peter off the slope. Luckily the rope linking him with the first guide caught on a projecting rock but the rope that connected him to the second guide snapped and this second guide fell to his death.

He used to visit his brother Walter in Finland and once, when about to sail for America, expressed regret that "the weather would not be rough to provide him with the full enjoyment of a sea-voyage." After Peter's death, Walter presented a bronze bust of his brother to Guy's and it can be seen today in the entrance hall of the Medical School.

One member of the family we ought not to forget is uncle Henry. After many years without any contact he sent a letter in 1884 to Joseph. He was writing from Texas. As a businessman he had not

172

made a success. He had been married three times and he was just preparing to get married again, to a widow.

Back in Farnworth, George T. Duffy passed on in 1870. Jamie was told. They had never exchanged a letter since they parted in 1863 but Jamie no longer expressed any bitter feeling towards him.

Of more interest perhaps is the fate of Martha J. Hamer. She named her little boy John. It came as a relief to James when he heard in the late 1860s that she was planning to get married. We find her in the spring of 1871 at 16, Barncroft Road, Farnworth, living next door to her mother. She had married a cotton mill operative, John Langshaw, and besides her own little son aged seven she had two children from the marriage: Eliza, aged two, and Samuel, a little baby. John Langshaw's brother, another mill operative, was also living with them.

Next door, at her mother's house, lived Selina. She was a widow now with two little children, a boy and a girl.

About 1895 Jamie eventually did come back to England, although only for a visit. It was a shortlived event for, when Martha heard of it, she began legal proceedings and Jamie hastily retreated back across the Atlantic.

As for little John Hamer, James always denied he was the father but his protests were not accepted by the family. As they watched the child grow they could see, as James could not, that he was the living image of their brother.

The Letters

THE HORROCKS LETTERS have survived in two collections and contain more than James's messages from the civil war. More than a hundred letters to William were spotted in a Manchester bookshop in 1958 and were forwarded to the Lancashire Record Office in Preston. The letters to William reproduced here have been published with the kind permission of the Lancashire County Archivist.

From Bank Cottage William moved across Bradshaw brook to live in a large stone building at the southern end of Chapeltown (Turton) High Street. Today it is the vicarage of the parish church. His daughters took great care of his former surgery equipment and it is thanks to them that these letters were preserved.

The bulk of the family's letters have come from Darwen. They were inherited from Joseph by Annie's daughters. In 1975 their home at 65, Richmond Terrace was sold and its contents auctioned. The letters, in a pine box, were bought by Keith Almond, an antique-dealer in Darwen, and formed part of his private collection of Darwen memorabilia. Four years later his collection, including the letters, was passed on to Blackburn Museum.

The earliest documents date from the beginning of the 1840s. The collection becomes fuller when William leaves home in 1859 for Guy's Medical School. He saved his parents' letters and his mother and father back in Farnworth preserved those from him. They describe operations and the life of a medical student.

As different offspring of the family left home, letters from them would be passed on to the next brother or sister so that each of the family could share the news. They became known among the Horrockses as the "Budget Letters". James's letters cover his days as a student in London as well as his adventures in America until he settles in St Louis. George's letters describe his travels around the world. Because several people are corresponding at the same time, the news from home tends to be similar for each one and therefore it

175

becomes possible to decipher a hidden reference in one person's letter by turning to another.

Fortunately Joseph kept a copy of the first letter, dated 25th August 1863, which he sent to James when James had joined the army. It tells of his mother's anxiety—the family had read in the press about rioting in New York and deaths caused by sunstroke in that city. There had also been a number of shipwrecks and the family were worried because Jamie had not written.

Believing James still to be in New York, Joseph told him that Messrs Barlow & Jones had asked if he would act as their agent.

We read that two weeks earlier Joseph had been invited to the wedding of cousin Rachel Horrocks and Robert Wood, but that when Bob Dearden's daughter, Mary Jane, married Peter Keeveny, the previous Wednesday, only William had been invited and he had refused.

Joseph's main message was this: "Up to the present moment we have had no tidings from you and mother especially is very dispirited."

In other letters we read about their father's ailments. He had been a sick man clearly long before the fatal accident at Bolton.

Preoccupations were preventing him from answering all James's letters, as can be seen from the following note he sent to Joseph:

23rd June 1864

My very dear Son Joseph,

Will you be kind enough to write upon this paper a letter to James giving him as much news as you can think of. I am so engaged I really cannot do it myself tho I will write something and have it ready by the end of this week when we shall meet again.

We have received by this eves post a thundering letter and newspaper from him. Eh! *Jemmy lad*.

Until we again meet, goodbye
George Horrocks

Joseph was acting as an anchor for the family. Three months later, on 8th September, he mentioned another letter to his father:

I have sent off my letter to James along with the photograph or carte de visite. I posted it on Tuesday and it would leave Liverpool by mail steamer on Wednesday.

After 1870 the surviving letters are few and far between. Of the 1860s, however, they provide a forceful account of the desires and adventures of a Lancashire family.

Appendix I

The Horrocks Family

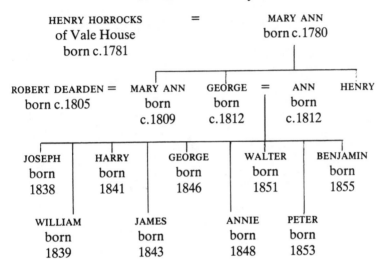

HENRY HORROCKS   =   MARY ANN
of Vale House   born c.1780
born c.1781

ROBERT DEARDEN =   MARY ANN   GEORGE   =   ANN   HENRY
born c.1805   born   born   born
                   c.1809   c.1812   c.1812

JOSEPH   HARRY   GEORGE   WALTER   BENJAMIN
born   born   born   born   born
1838   1841   1846   1851   1855

WILLIAM   JAMES   ANNIE   PETER
born   born   born   born
1839   1843   1848   1853

Appendix II

Officers & Engagements of the New Jersey Artillery Volunteers, 5th Battery
(taken from the *Record of Officers & Men of New Jersey in the Civil War, 1861–1865* by E S Stryker (Trenton, N.J., 1876))

No.	Name	Rank	Com. or Enrolled	Must'd In	Period
1	Zenas C Warren	Captain	8 Sept '63	8 Sept '63	3 Yrs
1	George F Durant	1st Lieut.	8 Sept '63	8 Sept '63	3 Yrs
2	Joseph Warren	1st Lieut.	19 Nov '63	10 Dec '63	3 Yrs
3	James Gillen	1st Lieut.	12 Feb '64	28 Mar '64	3 Yrs
1	Thomas R Perry	2nd Lieut	8 Sept '63	8 Sept '63	3 Yrs
2	James B Goldsmith	2nd Lieut.	8 Sept '63	2 Dec '63	3 Yrs
3	William Maxwell	2nd Lieut.	12 Feb '64	14 Mar '64	3 Yrs
4	Edward Chappell	2nd Lieut.	12 Feb '64	28 Mar '64	3 Yrs
1	James Fisher	1st Serj.	21 Aug '63	8 Sept '63	3 Yrs
1	Frederick Bishop	Qr. Mr. Serj.	19 Aug '63	8 Sept '63	3 Yrs
1	George Fisher	Sergeant	1 Jan '64	1 Jan '64	3 Yrs
2	William L Tomlinson	Sergeant	19 Oct '63	19 Oct '63	3 Yrs
3	Nicholas Relinger	Sergeant	1 Jan '64	1 Jan '64	3 Yrs
4	Lucas Henry	Sergeant	16 Feb '64	19 Feb '64	3 Yrs
5	Benedict Freeburg	Sergeant	16 Feb '64	19 Feb '64	3 Yrs
6	James Harold	Sergeant	20 Aug '63	8 Sept '63	3 Yrs
1	Patrick Hanratty	Corporal	21 Aug '63	8 Sept '63	3 Yrs
2	William Hartell	Corporal	15 Aug '63	8 Sept '63	3 Yrs
3	James P O'Neil	Corporal	30 Nov '63	1 Dec '63	3 Yrs
4	Charles F Neuber	Corporal	26 Feb '64	26 Feb '64	3 Yrs
5	Charles Goldbeck	Corporal	13 Feb '64	13 Feb '64	3 Yrs
6	William Hazens	Corporal	30 Dec '63	30 Dec '63	3 Yrs

(Warren)   12 June '65
(Durant)   Resigned Feb 6, '64
(Warren)   12 June '65   Serj. 1st Reg. N.Y. Mounted Rifles; Com. 1st Lieut. to
fill original vacancy.
(Gillen)   12 June '65   Private Oct 19, '63; Serj. Nov 12, '63; 2nd Lieut. Dec 12,
'63; 1st Lieut. vice Durant resigned.
(Perry)   Resigned Dec 11, '63.
(Goldsmith)   1st Serj. Co. E, 9th Reg; 2nd Lieut. to fill original
vacancy; resigned Feb 9, '64.
(Maxwell)   9 July '65   Private Aug 22, '63; Qr. Mr. Serj. Nov. 6, '63; 2nd Lieut.
vice Goldsmith resigned.
(Chappell)   Serj. Aug 21, '63; 2nd Lieut. vice Gillen promoted;
dismissed April 22, '65 absent without leave.
(Fisher)   12 June '65   Serj. Aug 21, '63; 1st Serj. March 28, '64; Com. 2nd
Lieut. May 28, '65, not mustered.
(Bishop)   12 June '65   Corp. Aug 19, '63; Private Sept 25, '63; Corp. Feb 10,
'64; Qr. Mr. Serj. May 30, '65.
(Fisher)   12 June '65   Recruit—Serj. Jan 27, '64.
(Tomlinson)   12 June '65   Recruit—Corp. Nov 6, '63; Serj. Dec 5, '63; Private Dec
29, '63; Guidon March 16, '64; Serj. May 4, '64.
(Relinger)   12 June '65   Recruit—Corp. Jan 27, '64; Serj. Feb 10, '64; Qr. Mr.
Serj. May 26, '64; Serj. Feb 19, '65.
(Henry)   12 June '65   Recruit—Corp. March 6, '64; Serj. May 10, '64.
(Freeburg)   12 June '65   Recruit—Corp. May 4, '64; Serj. July 16, '64.
(Harold)   12 June '65   Corp. April 18, '64; Serj. May 30, '65.
(Hanratty)   12 June '65   Corp. May 26, '64.
(Hartell)   12 June '65   Corp. Aug 15, '63; Serj. Oct 1, '63; Private Nov 6, '63;
Corp. Feb 10, '64.
(O'Neil)   12 June '65   Recruit—Transferred from Bat. A; Corp. June 5, '64.
(Neuber)   12 June '65   Recruit—Corp. July, 29, '64.
(Goldbeck)   12 June '65   Recruit—Corp. Dec 13, '64.
(Hazens)   12 June '65   Recruit—Transferred from Bat. A; Corp. Jan 10, '65.

Engagements
Howlett's House, Va.   9th May, 1864
Clover Hill Station, Va.   14th May, 1864
Drury's Bluff, Va.   15th May, 1864
Before Petersburg, Va.   8th June, 1864
Bermuda Hundred, Va.   16th June, 1864
Deep Bottom, Va.   27th July, 1864
Dutch Gap, Va.   13th Aug, 1864
Before Petersburg, Va.   2nd to 10th Sept, 1864
Darbytown Road, Va.   7th Oct, 1864
Capture of Richmond, Va.   3rd April, 1865

Index